The Dreams of Tipu Sultan

Bali: The Sacrifice

The Dreams of Tipu Sultan

'The [play] rescues Tipus from colonial perceptions and presents him refracted through history in a different perspective, that of independent India. More importantly the play is, in a collective sense, a reclamation of history, a truth too close to our heart for it to ever fail as a play.'

—Elizabeth Roy, *The Hindu*

Bali: The Sacrifice

'You have probably never seen anything quite like it. Drawing on myth to ask questions about religious tolerance and violence, it is both alien and completely accessible.

Nona Shepphard's canny, beautifully acted production offers both the simplicity of myth and a touch of Bollywood as tragedy and comedy, the universal and the deeply personal, spark off each other. Every time you are about to snort with laughter, you are stunned into silence by the realisation of what is at stake.

The experience is greater than the sum of its parts, and it is as enjoyable as it is thought-provoking.'

—Lynn Gardner, *The Guardian*

The Dreams of Tipu Sultan
Bali: The Sacrifice

Two Plays by GIRISH KARNAD

OXFORD
UNIVERSITY PRESS

OXFORD
UNIVERSITY PRESS

Oxford University Press is a department of the University of Oxford.
It furthers the University's objective of excellence in research, scholarship,
and education by publishing worldwide. Oxford is a registered trademark of
Oxford University Press in the UK and in certain other countries

Published in India by
Oxford University Press
22 Workspace, 2nd Floor, 1/22 Asaf Ali Road, New Delhi 110 002, India

© Oxford University Press 2004

First Edition published in 2004
Sixth impression 2015

ISBN-13: 978-0-19-566476-8
ISBN-10: 0-19-566476-0

Typeset in Minion 10.5/14
by Excellent Laser Typesetters, Pitampura, Delhi 110 034
Printed in India at Repro India Ltd

Photographs by Stephen Vaughan

Contents

THE DREAMS OF TIPU SULTAN

PREFACE

In 1996, the BBC commissioned me to write a radio play to celebrate the Fiftieth Anniversary of Indian Independence. The plot obviously had to deal with some aspect of Indo-British relations and I immediately thought of Tipu Sultan, one of the most politically perceptive and tragic figures in modern Indian history. It was the late A.K. Ramanujan who drew my attention to the record of his dreams maintained by this warrior.

Tipu has always fascinated playwrights. *Tipu Saib or British Valour in India* was put on at Covent Garden, London, as early as 1791 and was followed by a series of spectaculars. In Karnataka, Tipu has continued to inspire folk ballads and I have, in my lifetime, seen three Kannada stage versions of his life, two of them by itinerant troupes of rural actors.

The radio play was broadcast by the BBC on 15 August 1997 and was directed by Jatinder Verma of Tara Arts with Saeed Jaffrey playing Tipu Sultan. Karnataka Nataka Rangayana, the state repertory, staged the Kannada version in the precinct of Daria Daulat, Tipu's summer palace in Srirangapatna, to commemorate his 200th death anniversary in May 1999. It was directed by C. Basavalingaiah, with Hulugappa Kattimani in the lead role.

The present text has been entirely rewritten for the stage.

Bangalore   GIRISH KARNAD

NOTE

Those who wish to stage the play should kindly resist the temptation of using masks, special lighting or costumes for the dream scenes. It is essential for the total impact of the play that the dreams are staged absolutely realistically, and that the scenes follow each other in rapid succession. As this rapidity can be best achieved by quick shifts of location on stage and of lighting, exits and entrances of characters have not always been indicated in the text in the traditional fashion.

The Dreams of Tipu Sultan was first presented by the Madras Players at the YMCA Amphitheatre, Chennai, on 17 February 2000. The principal cast was as follows:

TONY PICKFORD	Colin Mackenzie
HARSHA SUBRAMANIAM	Hussain Ali Kirmani
RAVI KATARI	Mark Wilks
P. VENKAT	Zafer
JASPER UTLEY	Arthur Wellesley
VIKRAM GOPALAKRISHNAN	Nadeem Khan
ASIM SHARMA	Tipu Sultan
T. T. SRINATH	Poornaiya
RUPA BOSE	Female Idols
MALA GOVIAS	
P. VENKAT	Old Men
BRIAN PAPALLI	
GAUTHAM ADITHYA	Mir Sadiq
PAUL MATHEW	Ghulam Ali Khan
EJJI UMAMAHESH	Osman Khan
P. VENKAT	
SIDDHARTH CHOUDHRY	Fath Haidar
SUKRIT CHOUDHRY	Muizuddin
MADHULICA SUNDARAM	Abdul Khaliq
ANURADHA ANANTH	Young Man

JIM HODGETTS	Charles Malet
ARYAMA SUNDARAM	Nana Phadnavis
SRIYA CHARI	Ruqayya Banu
SUMIKA MUKERJI	Hasina
RANJAN DE	Lord Cornwallis
JAGAN R.	Qamaruddin
VENKY NAIK	Haidar Ali
ARUN MANI	Hari Pant
TONY PICKFORD	Lord Mornington (Richard Wellesley)
JIM HODGETTS	William Kirkpatrick
Directed by	N.S. YAMUNA
Sets and lights by	M. NATESH

Act One

1803. The house of the historian, Mir Hussain Ali Khan Kirmani, in the city of Mysore. Colonel Colin Mackenzie, the Oriental scholar, is taking off his shoes, as though he has just arrived. He looks around at the notes, books, and manuscripts littering the floor.
Kirmani enters with a jug of water and a tumbler, and places them next to Mackenzie.

MACKENZIE: How's the work progressing?

KIRMANI: Not at all well.

MACKENZIE: Why not?

KIRMANI: It's not easy. It hurts.

MACKENZIE: That's what you keep saying, Janaab Kirmani. But come now—after all these years—

KIRMANI: There's no healing. True, the blood and the tears dried up a long time ago. But the wound remains fresh.

MACKENZIE: That's understandable. I mean, you *were* close to him. But you are also a historian. You need to develop a certain objectivity—

KIRMANI: Yes, that's what you keep telling me, Mackenzie Sahib. Objectivity. Dispassionate distance. Is that even possible?

MACKENZIE: Essential, I'd say. A must.

KIRMANI: Then perhaps you should dismiss me. You pay me to write history while I malinger and mope...

MACKENZIE: I didn't mean that. In any case, you know you are irreplaceable, you old rascal! One can't buy genuine court historians in the bazaar.

KIRMANI: Perhaps you think malingering is a courtier's disease?

MACKENZIE: No, I don't. I think you're far too obsessed with his death.

KIRMANI: Not his death. The way he was destroyed.

MACKENZIE: Surely you're being melodramatic now. Every bit of evidence we've gathered proves he asked for it.

KIRMANI: Yes. For you, he's made up of bits of evidence, bits of argument that prove that your side was right. And that's what I don't understand. You have your version of history, all worked out. Why do you want my side? Why do you care?

MACKENZIE: I am interested in the other side. You could say that's how we Europeans are brought up...to be interested in the other side as well. That I suppose is our strength.

KIRMANI: I find a lifetime insufficient to understand my own. Besides I spent my life serving him and his father. And now I work for you, his enemies. What does that make me? A traitor? Am I trustworthy any more? Doesn't that worry you? It worries me.

MACKENZIE: Our loyalty is to history, Kirmaniji. Keep emotion out. Stick to the facts.

KIRMANI: You mean, memories. But that's where the real betrayal lies. Do you know I was just trying to remember what he looked like on that last day and I just couldn't.

MACKENZIE: That's another thing you have avoided writing about. His last day.

KIRMANI: I remember it vividly. But the crucial detail still eludes me. He was staying in the caravanserai on the northern ramparts. He'd been there for a couple of days, with the soldiers, watching the English noose tighten. It was sweltering hot. We had been praying for a downpour, for then the moats would have been flooded and the English attack delayed. But the clouds had hung ominously, inert, neutral. We were half-way through our lunch, our sweat streaming into our plates, when the skies exploded. The English had launched their assault. The Sultan washed his fingers and got up. He buckled on his sword belt, took out an envelope from his pocket, sealed it and gave it to me: 'Keep it till I come back,' he said. At that moment, news came that Syed Gaffar had been killed by a cannonball. He mumbled a prayer and left. I remember thinking, I'll never forget that expression on his face. But I have. For the life of me, I can't remember his face at that moment. It's such ... such betrayal!

MACKENZIE: And then?

KIRMANI: I forgot all about the letter. Naturally, with all that followed. Next day, I found it in my pocket. Reluctantly, I broke open the seal. Inside was a paper on which he had recorded the dream he had had the previous night. His last dream. With that my history ends. Yours begins. (*Pause.*)

MACKENZIE: I saw him first in the flickering light of a torch. Still warm. We thought he was alive, buried deep under a pile of corpses. Near the water gate of the fort. The night of the fourth of May, 1799.

(*Ramparts of the Seringapatam—or Srirangapatna—fort. Midnight. There has been savage fighting and the ground is thick with the bodies of the dead and the dying. British soldiers are searching through the piles of bodies for Tipu's corpse. Tipu's servants, brought in to help identify his body, squat around, dozing.*)

SOLDIER 1: Is that him?

SOLDIER 2: Could be. No way one can be certain.

CAPT. WILKS: Corpulent, with big twirly moustaches, round face...

SOLDIER 2: Yes, sir. We know that by heart now. But the description seems to fit most of these bastards.

WILKS: Ask that black there.

SOLDIER 3: Look, sir, I'm sure we're wasting our time. I'm sure the bird's flown. He would be stupid not to—

WILKS (*ignores him*): Ask him.

SOLDIER 2: Is there any point, sir? These swine have already identified a dozen corpses as the Sultan's—they're making fools of us.

WILKS: Ask the one huddled in the right corner of the group. We haven't tried him.

SOLDIER 2: *Arre suno—Tum naheen—Han! Tum!* (You there! Not you—Yes, you!)

ZAFER: *Jee Huzoor.*

SOLDIER 2: *Yehan aao.* (Come here.)

ZAFER: *Jee.*

SOLDIER 2: *Naam kya hai?* (Name?)

ZAFER: Zafer.

SOLDIER 2: *Yeh murdah. Kya yeh tumhare Sultan ka hai?* (This corpse. Is it your Sultan's?)

ZAFER: *Dikhai naheen de rahaa… Andhera.* (Can't see… It's dark.)

SOLDIER 2: He says he can't see in the dark.

WILKS: True enough. Why haven't the torches arrived? Halloo—Ricketts—

VOICE (*distant*): Sah!

WILKS: Where are the torches? We can't see a damn thing here.

VOICE: On their way I suppose, sah—

WILKS: You suppose, do you? Thanks. Send your torch here.

VOICE: A moment, sah. We may have something here.

WILKS: So may we. So send it here. On the double.

SOLDIER 3: It's bloody ridiculous. We fight and kill these devils through the day. Then sift their rotting bodies through the night. Like scavengers.

SOLDIER 1: A dozen teams scavenging and three torches between them.

VOICE: More torches and flares coming, sah. And it's Colonel Wellesley, sah.

WELLESLEY (*from a distance*): Hello! Captain Wilks—

WILKS: Here, sir.

WELLESLEY (*from a distance*): Where are you, Mark?

WILKS: Near the water gate, sir. Could you bring some torches and flares with you, sir?

(*Colonel Arthur Wellesley enters with a group of soldiers carrying torches. The torches are distributed.*)

WELLESLEY: This surely is what hell is like!

WILKS: It's Tipu's men, sir. They wouldn't yield. It was carnage.

SOLDIER 1: It's hot as hell too.

WILKS: We've had it if it rains now.

WELLESLEY: Even without the rains, it should not take long before they begin to stink. And the city must be getting restive. They'll want their dead. Let's hope we find him soon. Apparently he was last seen around here.

SOLDIER 3: If I may say so, sir, if the bastard's really lying dead somewhere here, we should let him rot in the sun—feed him to the dogs!

WELLESLEY: I understand how you feel. But we can't leave any corpse unturned, you understand.

WILKS (*laughs*): Of course not, sir.

WELLESLEY: We've got to decide whether Tipu is dead or in hiding or has run away before we can take the next step. Colonel Mackenzie should be here soon with the Manager of the Fort. But we must carry on in the meantime.

WILKS: Would you like to see some fun, sir?
(*Pointing to Zafer*)
    Ask him, Jones.

SOLDIER 2: *Aao, dekho. Inko pehchante ho?* (Come and look. Do
    you recognize him?)
(*Holds a torch to a dead body. Zafer looks and begins to wail.*)

ZAFER: *Han! Han! Yehee hain hamare padshah! Yehi hain—Allah!*
    Ab kya hoga?

SOLDIER 2 (*resigned*): He says, yes. It's the Sultan.

WILKS: While the others sit on their haunches and watch calmly
    from a distance?

SOLDIER 3: Why don't we kick the bastards? They aren't even
    trying to fool us!

WELLESLEY: Can't blame them.

WILKS: All right. Pile that body along with the others.

SOLDIER 3: I'll take any bet Tipu's run away, his tail between
    his legs.

SOLDIER 2 (*laughs*): We'll take bets when we're done with the
    city. You'll have something to bet with then.

SOLDIER 3: I can barely wait to lay my hands on it. I was a
    prisoner here. I've seen the city. Plated with gold, it is.

WILKS: Stop counting your chickens and get on with the bloody
    job.

VOICE (*distant*): Halloo—Is Colonel Wellesley there?

WELLESLEY (*shouts back*): Here! Near the water gate. Is that you,
    Colin?

MACKENZIE (*entering along with Nadeem Khan*): This is Qilledar
    Nadeem Khan, Manager of the Fort. Colonel Wellesley.

WELLESLEY: Delighted to meet you, sir. I wish the circumstances
    were more pleasant.

NADEEM: It's God's will.

WELLESLEY: We'd be grateful for your assistance.

NADEEM: It's my duty to the Sultan. I saw him last here, fighting like a man possessed.

WELLESLEY: Is it likely that Tipu Sultan might have escaped?

NADEEM: That wouldn't be like him. Besides, all the gates of the fort were closed.
(*Pause.*)
    I had seen to that.
(*Neither Wellesley nor Mackenzie react.*)
    If you'll permit me—
(*He starts looking for Tipu's body.*)

WELLESLEY: What news of the palace, Colin? All well, I presume.

MACKENZIE: They surrendered all right. There was no resistance. The princes took their time coming out; they were shaking with fright. General Baird became a little impatient—

WELLESLEY: Let me guess the rest.

MACKENZIE: Nothing serious. He cooled down soon enough.

WELLESLEY: Hm! Any trace of the Sultan?

MACKENZIE: He's not in the palace. They say he left two days ago. Has been camping out with the soldiers, somewhere on the ramparts.

NADEEM: Sahib—*Yeh hain*—Raja Khan—

SOLDIER 2 (*excited*): Nadeem Khan's found Raja Khan, the Sultan's personal assistant.
(*They run.*)

MACKENZIE: That means Tipu's body must be somewhere around? Where, Qilledar Sahib? There? Move these bodies. The lot. Look sharp.

SOLDIER 2: *Jaldi—Jaldi*—(Quick! Quick!)

NADEEM: *Thehro! Yeh hain*—(Stop. That's him!)

MACKENZIE: I think we've found him. Careful. That one with the gold buckle on his belt. Lift him out.

WILKS (*shouts*): We have found him. Bring all the torches here.

VOICES (*distant*): You have?—That's bloody marvellous—They've found him—Where?

(*Commotion. Soldiers come running and crowd around the body.*)

WELLESLEY: Steady now. Form a circle and hold your torches close to him. Is that Tipu Sultan, Qilledar Sahib?

NADEEM (*broken voice*): *Jee han.*

WELLESLEY: So that's the Tiger of Mysore.

SOLDIER 2: He's warm.

WELLESLEY: Is he alive?

(*Feels Tipu's temperature.*)

MACKENZIE: Is he?

WELLESLEY: He is warm, but that wound on his temple. Couldn't have survived that.

(*A chorus of voices, mainly female, is heard wailing in the far distance. They listen.*)

WELLESLEY (*listening*): But what's that?

MACKENZIE: That's from the palace—The harem—

WELLESLEY: The ladies of the palace mourning!

MACKENZIE: But how could they have known so soon? The palace is a mile away.

WILKS: Some secret signal.

WELLESLEY: In this dark?

MACKENZIE: It's eerie.

WELLESLEY: If we were looking for confirmation, I suppose that's it—

(*The wailing gets louder and spreads. The entire city is soon wailing.*)

SOLDIER 3 (*eagerly*): Is the city ours then, sir?

WELLESLEY: I suppose I can't stop you.
(*The soldiers rush out, hurrahing, eager to plunder the city.*)
   The only thing more melancholy than losing a battle is winning it. Mark—

WILKS: Yes, sir.

WELLESLEY: Get the body moved to the palace. And keep watch.

WILKS: Yes, sir.
(*They move away discussing the details.*)

SOLDIER 1: Excuse me, sir.

MACKENZIE: Yes?

SOLDIER 1: May I borrow your penknife, sir? I lost mine in the action.

MACKENZIE: Penknife? Certainly. Here.

SOLDIER 1: Thank you, sir. Before the body is taken away, I mean. I'd promised my friend Dr Cruso of our Establishment a present—
(*Chops off one of Tipu's moustaches.*)

MACKENZIE (*shouts*): What are you doing, man? What in the name of the Devil are you doing? Stop that lunatic—
(*Exclamations of horror, not too loud, in Urdu and Kannada. 'Arre—Roko—Ayyo! Ayyo! Yeh kya kiya?'*)

SOLDIER 1: The tiger's own whiskers. A prize booty.

MACKENZIE: Arrest that damned fool!
(*The sounds of wailing grow louder and merge with the shouts and screams of the city being pillaged. The sound track is entirely taken over by the latter. We are back in Kirmani's house.*)

KIRMANI: So the Tiger of Mysore had at last been hunted down. And the first salutation he received from the hunters was to have his whiskers chopped off.

MACKENZIE: That act of vandalism will not be forgotten.

KIRMANI: How could it be? It was a perfect prelude to a night of unprecedented rapacity.

MACKENZIE: I had never seen British soldiers go berserk like that!

KIRMANI: Every house looted. Every available woman raped. Soldiers throwing away precious jewellery because they could not carry any more.

MACKENZIE: Wellesley had to hang three soldiers before the pillage died down. Dreadful! Well, I'd better get back to my Sanskrit. The *Arthasastra*. The Science of Governance. A cynical piece of writing, if there ever was one. Get over your despondency, old man, and get on with your writing.

KIRMANI: I'll try. But I don't know what to write.

MACKENZIE: For the hundredth time, Kirmaniji, I wish you would write about Tipu's embassy to Mauritius—the Malarctic adventure. It proved to be his undoing and yet we don't have enough details.

KIRMANI: It never happened.

MACKENZIE: There! I can't understand it! It wasn't half as bad as the other things he did. Like trying to befriend Napoleon. Governor Malarctic is insignificant, an eminently forgettable Frenchman, if he hadn't caused Tipu's downfall. Yet you keep denying the whole thing. Why?

KIRMANI: Colonel Sahib, what you call the Malarctic Deal never happened.

MACKENZIE (*resigned*): If you insist. But Lord Mornington had absolute proof of Tipu's mischief.

KIRMANI: Perhaps His Lordship was dreaming.

MACKENZIE: I beg your pardon, Kirmaniji. Are you accusing the Governor General of India of lying?

KIRMANI: How could I, Colonel Sahib? I am employed by the Honourable John Company. But dreaming is not dishonourable. My master, Tipu Sultan, dreamt.

MACKENZIE: I know. And kept a record! By the way, what happened to his last dream?

KIRMANI: The night he was buried, a thunderstorm burst over Seringapatam.

MACKENZIE: Ah, yes! I remember. A deluge of extraordinary violence—two of our men were killed—

KIRMANI: Doors and windows in the city had already been torn down by the British soldiers. Most houses were roofless. And now, through the night, the rain lashed with a fury that made the soldiers' rampage seem like child's play. It destroyed all my papers. Wiped away every word written in ink. Within a night, all my recorded facts became memory.

MACKENZIE: Pity!

KIRMANI: Nature did with *that* dream what Munshi Habibullah should have done with the rest.

MACKENZIE: What do you mean?

KIRMANI: Munshi Habibullah was a fool. He should have destroyed the diary, when he found it.

MACKENZIE: There was no harm in it.

KIRMANI: It was a diary in which my master had recorded his dreams. He had kept it concealed from his closest confidants. I didn't know of its existence. None of us did. I couldn't believe my eyes when I saw the words written on its first page, in the Sultan's own hand.

(*Suddenly Tipu's voice is heard. But only Kirmani reacts to it.*)

TIPU'S VOICE: In this register are recorded the dreams I've had and am having.

KIRMANI: The Sultan had hidden the diary under his pillow and there it had lain after his death…until that idiot Munshi stumbled on it. It was sacred, personal.

MACKENZIE: I'm afraid we merely saw it as an odd little book. A pleasantly inconsequential conversation piece. (*Ironic.*) An ideal gift for the Chairman of the Court of Directors of the Honourable East India Company.

KIRMANI (*almost to himself*): There were blank pages in the diary. What dreams Tipu meant to record there and why he didn't will never be known.

MACKENZIE: Blank pages in a secret record of dreams—that's Tipu for you.

KIRMANI: Evidently, Colonel Colin Mackenzie Sahib, he recorded the dreams that spoke to him.
(*Pause.*)

And some probably didn't.

MACKENZIE (*laughs*): Janaab Hussain Ali Kirmani Sahib. I am interested in the people who spoke to him and the ones he spoke to. You keep the dreams to yourself.

KIRMANI (*smiling*): I will too.
(*From now on, Kirmani and Mackenzie act as choric characters, commenting on the action, as indicated. The stage darkens. Tipu enters, accompanied by Poornaiya.*)

TIPU: On the 3rd day of the month of Thamari, the last night of the month of Ramzan followed next morning by Idd in the year of Dalw 1213 from the birth of the Prophet, I was returning with my army from Farrukhi near Salamabad when I had the following dream. I had been on an elephant shikar and on my way back was walking with Poornaiya, the Finance Minister, when we saw a big temple. It was in a dilapidated state, and I said: 'Poornaiya, look at that structure. It looks quite mysterious.'

POORNAIYA: Yes, Your Majesty. It does indeed.

TIPU: Let's go in and have a look.
(*Lights come on to show a strange building with several human images.*)

Poornaiya, what idols are these? Are they some gods you recognize?

POORNAIYA: No, Your Majesty. I don't think they are gods.

TIPU: They don't seem to belong to any religion I know.

POORNAIYA: They are strange. I have never seen such figures before.

TIPU: Look, Poornaiya—look—their eyes! They are moving. These stone images are moving their eyes!

POORNAIYA: Let's go back, sir. This darkness has a malevolence about it. We'd better get out—

TIPU: No, let's go on. Let's inspect them more closely.

POORNAIYA: Be careful, sir. Those two. They are getting up. Look out!

(*Two women in the last row stand up. They are wearing nine-yard saris. One of them pulls her sari up between her knees.*)

TIPU: Who are you? Are you human or are you some spirits?

WOMAN: Your Majesty, we are living women. The rest of us, these men here, are merely images. We have been here for many centuries now, praying to God and seeking our salvation.

TIPU: Good. I'm sorry then we've disturbed you. Do you need any help?

WOMAN: None at all except for total isolation.

TIPU: So be it. Ladies, keep yourselves occupied with thoughts of God. Come, Poornaiya. Let's go. We'll have the temple repaired, the walls rebuilt so that these seekers after God are not disturbed.

POORNAIYA: As Your Majesty wishes.

(*They walk out of the temple when two old men, with long beards, in flowing silk gowns, approach them. Beside them are two elephants and several footmen carrying spears and guns.*)

OLD MAN: Greetings to Your Majesty.

TIPU: Greetings! Who are you? You seem to have come from a long distance.

OLD MAN: We are the envoys of the Emperor of China.

TIPU: Please enter and take a seat in the Diwan-i-Aam. What is the object of your visit?

OLD MAN: We wish nothing but the promotion of greater friendship. The Emperor of China sends you a white elephant and these horses as a token of his friendship and affection for you.

TIPU: The elephants and horses are indeed beautiful. I am deeply touched. I am also eager to know how you capture and train elephants in China. Besides, I know from Hadrat Nizami's book, *Sikandar-namah*, that the Emperor of China had sent a present of a white elephant, a horse, and a female slave to the Great Alexander.

OLD MAN: Yes indeed. The Emperor has never sent a white elephant to anyone except the Great Alexander and now to Your Presence.

(*Tipu addresses the audience while the others on stage are enveloped in darkness.*)

TIPU: In the meantime morning dawned and I rose. My interpretation of the dream is that God Almighty and our Prophet will make me another Alexander...

(*He moves to the Diwan-i-khas and holds a conference with Mir Sadiq and Poornaiya.*)

...and the many faiths in my Kingdom will depend upon me for protection and succour.

POORNAIYA: As indeed they do.

TIPU: Have another kebab, Mir Sadiq.

MIR SADIQ: No, thank you, Your Majesty. The kebabs are delicious, which I have already proved by my enormous appetite.

TIPU: Poornaiya, another apple?

POORNAIYA: Your Majesty is most generous. But I must decline.

TIPU: From Kashmir, as you know. A rare delicacy in south India. You shouldn't refuse—

POORNAIYA: Its texture is so exquisite and the colouring so delicate that it is a supreme pleasure just to look at it.

TIPU: Like a woman's…

(*Pause.*)

…cheeks?

(*Laughter.*)

So where were we? Ah, yes! To the list drawn up for our delegation, add silkworms and eggs from the island of Jezeriah Diraz near Muscat—

MIR SADIQ: But the ones we got from China are doing very well, sir. Do we need—

TIPU: Of course we need others. These may be better. I'm told they are better suited to our climatic conditions. Five or six men who know the proper mode of rearing the worms will need to be brought along with them. All right, what next?

MIR SADIQ: The letter from Raja Ramchander.

TIPU: Oh, that one! He is an ass.

MIR SADIQ: Your Majesty, I think he has a point. He says the idea of shops and warehouses owned by the Government is scaring the traders off. They are actually moving to customers who are poorer—

TIPU (*impatient*): Oh, will none of you ever learn? If profits are only seven pagodas while the expenses on clerks and accountants come to ten, how can anyone survive in business? How long will these traders be able to carry their bullion to other places? Don't you worry! They'll come back to us—crawling.

POORNAIYA: What the Honourable Mir Sadiq means, I think, is that it's not the economics that scares the traders. It's the idea of dealing with the Government, particularly the idea of the Government turning into a trading agency.

TIPU (*exploding*): Then they'd better like it. And both of you too! We need glass. We need guns. We need cannons. Shall we keep buying them from abroad? Even for that we need money. And shall we be content with the pittance we get by taxing our businessmen when we have ivory and sandalwood freely available? Can an individual trader deal in sandalwood? For centuries we begged and borrowed silk from the Chinese. And everyone predicted disaster when I got a few eggs from China. And now we have a flourishing industry of our own. Shall we sit back like the stupid Nizam and the Marathas who continue as though the English never existed—indeed, as though the Europeans never existed? Any other mail?

MIR SADIQ: None of importance.

TIPU: Good. Have the Honourable Ghulam Ali Khan and others arrived?

MIR SADIQ: They wait in the audience chamber.

TIPU: That's the Noble Ghulam Ali for you. Always on time—like a European. Send them in. And where are my sons?

MIR SADIQ: Their Persian teacher must be here.

TIPU: Would you please send for them? The teacher can wait. I want my sons to be present when I talk to the delegation. It's time they started learning about the world.

(*Mir Sadiq signals to a servant who departs to fetch the children. Ghulam Ali Khan and Osman Khan enter.*)

OSMAN KHAN: May the Lord protect Your Majesty.

TIPU: Welcome, welcome, Honourable Osman Khan, Ghulam Ali Khan. I hope your families are well.

GHULAM ALI KHAN: God's mercy and your diligence look after them.

(*Fath Haidar, aged around ten, Muizuddin and Abdul Khaliq, just short of six, enter and bow to those present.*)

TIPU: Ah, Fath Haidar, Muizuddin, Abdul Khaliq! Come and sit down and listen carefully. Pay attention to everything. You know these noblemen.

PRINCES: Yes, Father. We bow to you, Uncles.

OSMAN KHAN: May God's grace be on you.

TIPU: Let me come to the point without further ado. We wish
to send a delegation to France. You know Monsieur Pierre
Monneron, from Pondicherry. Through his good offices we
have arranged with the French Governor General of Mauritius
for a visit by a royal delegation of Mysore to France. The
Governor General has agreed to talk to the King of France
and arrange an audience. Gentlemen, I want you to go on
that delegation. Honourable Osman Khan, you'll lead it.

OSMAN KHAN: This is indeed an honour—

GHULAM ALI KHAN: We shall be the envy of the world.

TIPU: Actually, how I wish I could go with you. I envy you!

OSMAN KHAN: Your Majesty would certainly have proved a better
leader of the delegation than I and the King of France would
have been happier to deal with a quicker intelligence.

TIPU: Go on, go on. Make fun of me. What else am I here for?
But they say in the sea off Mauritius, you can actually see
the seven colours of the rainbow. Then Paris, Versailles! You
are going on a fairy-tale voyage. I envy you. But unlike you,
I am not a free man.

(*Laughter. Roar of tigers is heard in the background.*)

TIPU: Why are the tigers restless? Have they been fed?

SERVANT: Yes, Your Majesty. It's that Bahadur Khan—he's noisy.

TIPU: He is growing up. He needs more food than the others.
Tell that to the zoo-keeper.

SERVANT: Yes, Your Majesty.

(*The children suppress their laughter.*)

TIPU: What's funny?

(*The children fall suddenly silent.*)

What's so funny?

FATH: The tigers become restless this time every day. And every day you give the same instruction.

(*Laughter. Tipu playfully growls at his children. Then turns to the delegation.*)

Your main objective is to explain to the King of France the situation in India. Particularly the state of the French here.

OSMAN KHAN: Yes, Your Majesty.

TIPU: I'll give you a letter for King Louis the XVI. But a letter is no substitute for direct persuasion. You must convince the King that if the French don't wake up, the English will gobble up the whole of India. The French here have become listless. The King must prod them, kick them if necessary into activity. Louis and I could sign a Treaty of Perpetual Alliance. Then if ten thousand French soldiers could march under me—under me, make that clear, no separate treaties with the British or the other Indian princes, I give the orders—if the King could give me that little, we could change the face of India. Do you understand?

GHULAM ALI KHAN: We do, Your Majesty.

TIPU: When you return, bring with you, not just the ten thousand soldiers, but French craftsmen who could make guns, cannons, pistols.

OSMAN KHAN: Yes, Your Majesty.

TIPU: You know that the delegation we sent to Istanbul last year to His Holiness the Caliph of All Islamic Nations proved a sensational success. Turkey, Arabia, Iran—they are all clamouring for our products.

MIR SADIQ: The Imam of Muscat has fallen in love with the sandalwood and spices of our land and permitted us to build a factory for our products there.

TIPU: So that's what you've got to look for—opportunities for business! It'll benefit them and of course us. Soldiers, yes, but trade, industry, money. I've made a provisional list of professionals we'll need. Poornaiya, read out the list so they can think about it.

POORNAIYA: A doctor, a surgeon, a smelter, a carpenter, a weaver, a blacksmith, a locksmith, a cutter…

MUIZ: And a watch-maker, Father.

TIPU: It's there, son. It's there.

POORNAIYA: A dyer. A watch-maker.

FATH: And a gardener, Father?

TIPU (*delighted*): You see, I have geniuses for sons. And they know what I've in mind. Do you think I would have forgotten a gardener?

POORNAIYA: I have not included a gardener, Your Majesty. We have many of our own.

TIPU: No, no, no. We must have someone from there. We need new ideas. Two gardeners. From the garden of Versailles. They'll work in our Lal Bagh.

FATH: They should bring new varieties of trees, flowers and bushes.

OSMAN: We shall endeavour to bring every item of interest we come across, Your Highness.

TIPU: You must, you must indeed. That's what makes Europe so wonderful—it's full of new ideas—inventions—all kinds of machines—bursting with energy. Why don't we in our country think like them? I've just read about something called a ther-mo-meter. You must bring me one.

GHULAM ALI KHAN: I beg your pardon, sir?

TIPU: Ther-mo-meter! It is quicksilver in a glass tube. When placed in the hands of a sick man, the quicksilver rises to a certain number of degrees and indicates the height of his disorder. That helps the *hakim* decide on the treatment.

POORNAIYA: Pardon me, sir. But can such a thing be possible?

TIPU: Ah! Poornaiya, the sceptic! He believes his ancestors knew everything that could possibly be known and that there's nothing new left to discover.

POORNAIYA: I look forward to seeing this wonderful instrument, Your Majesty.

TIPU: Which means, my dear princes, that he doesn't believe my word. Well, I'm told there's a whole book on that subject. We should get it translated into Persian.

MIR SADIQ: It'll be done the moment I receive a copy.

TIPU: But no self-indulgence. No slacking. This is not a picnic. Please bear that in mind. I'm told the city of Paris enchants people like a woman, and they forget themselves in its embrace. Whenever you feel lazy or despondent, think of the John Company—how they came to this country, poor, cringing, and what they have become in a mere fifty years. They threaten us today. It's all because of their passion for trade.

OSMAN KHAN: We shall do our best, Your Majesty.

TIPU: Good then. Start preparing for your journey. The Chief Astrologer of Chennapatna has chosen four days within the next three months on which the stars are propitious. We've sent the dates to Pondicherry and the French will let us know on which of those days a ship of theirs is scheduled to sail for Mauritius.

GHULAM ALI KHAN: This is like a dream come true, Your Majesty.

OSMAN KHAN: We can barely wait for that day.

TIPU: Be with your families till then. Be affectionate to your children, loving to your wives. You'll not see them for a couple of years.

(*Laughter.*)

May God be with you.

OSMAN KHAN: With your permission, Your Majesty.

(*The delegation withdraws.*)

TIPU: So what do you think of that, Sons?

FATH: What a marvellous idea, Father! We'll stun the world! Father—

TIPU: Yes?

FATH: Can't I join the delegation?

TIPU: And what about your studies here?

FATH: I'll learn on the way. Uncles will teach me. Besides you always say grandfather couldn't even read and write and yet—

TIPU: And was therefore foul-mouthed. You have to prepare for a different world. Go now. Your teacher must be waiting.

MUIZ: How long will it take the French troops to come, Father? Can I march with them into battle?

TIPU: Let's hope they don't take that long.
(*Laughter.*)

Off you go!
(*The children bow and go out.*)

POORNAIYA: If they come at all, Your Majesty. Forgive me for saying so but the English and the French have signed a treaty in Versailles, by which neither is allowed to enter into the local affairs in India.

TIPU (*thoughtful*): You may be right. But I keep hoping. After all, the French and the English are neighbours—they can't be friends for ever. They are bound to start quarrelling. We can't live from moment to moment, without a plan of action, Poornaiya, although the Nizam has proved that even that can be done.

MIR SADIQ: But the recent reports from Madras suggest that the English may be in a friendlier mood now.

TIPU: They have puppets in Madras. We need to keep our ears tuned to Calcutta. That's the Capital, after all.

POORNAIYA: The new Governor General, one gathers, has been

specially instructed by the Board of Control not to get into trouble with us.

TIPU: Ah! Pitt's India Act! The 'Leave-India-alone' Act! Do you believe a word of it? Do you think if the English wanted peace they would have appointed Lord Cornwallis as the Governor General?

POORNAIYA: We're told he is a wise, upright man—

TIPU: And a defeated General! Poornaiya, you are a Brahmin. You ride a horse and lead a battalion, but you think like a pedant. You do not understand a soldier. This man Cornwallis—he led the English armies in the Americas and he lost the war! To a farmer called Washington! And his Government sends him to India—

POORNAIYA: Let's pray that he understands Peace, Your Majesty.

TIPU: He understands nothing but the ignominy of defeat, of surrender. Can't you imagine the whispers, the sly smiles, the nudges that must have greeted the Lord in London? Even if no slights were intended, he would have imagined them. He must, if he is a soldier! Can't you see him tossing and turning in bed, thinking only of refurbishing his honour? And he knows—and I know—that to get the stain off his reputation he needs to vanquish one man in India—only one—Tipu Sultan!

(*Pause.*)

His appointment is as sure a pointer as the conjuction of Saturn and Mars in the third sector of Aries. We'll soon have the shadow of the English falling across our doorstep.

(*The stage darkens. Tipu turns to the audience.*)

TIPU: On the sixth day of the Khusrawi month in the year of Busd, as I was preparing for a night attack on the Maratha armies of Hari Pant Phadke at Shahnur near Devgiri, I had a dream.

(*A young man, turbaned like a Maratha, enters.*)

A handsome young man, fair-skinned and light-eyed, approached me and I said: 'Who are you, young man? Why don't you speak?'

YOUNG MAN (*female voice*): You are very handsome, Your Majesty.

TIPU: Thank you. Come. Come and sit by me.

YOUNG MAN: But I'm not telling you anything you don't already know.

TIPU: Well, it's always nice to be reminded. When one spends as much time on horseback as I do, there's no time to look into mirrors.

YOUNG MAN: But surely your *begums* tell you. Specially Ruqayya Banu, your favourite queen—

TIPU: Beware! You're being impertinent.

YOUNG MAN: It's my intense admiration for you that makes me so bold—

TIPU: Look, I'm not given to entering into such conversation with just anyone.

YOUNG MAN: But I'm not just anyone.

TIPU: Then who are you?

YOUNG MAN: Doesn't anything strike you as unusual about me?

TIPU: Oh! Several things. You're delicate looking. And you have a woman's voice.

(*The young man bows in front of Tipu.*)

YOUNG MAN: Will the Sarkar-e-Khudadad kindly take off my turban?

(*Tipu takes off the turban and a cascade of long hair comes tumbling down on the shoulders of the youth. He then stands with his back to the audience, facing Tipu.*)

YOUNG MAN: Will you unbutton my blouse, Your Majesty?

(*Pause.*)

You're blushing. You have gone red. I didn't realize Your Majesty is such a shy man. Let me do that for you, sir... Here!

(*Unbuttons the blouse. Tipu reacts.*)

TIPU: You are a woman! Why are you in this disguise?

YOUNG MAN: I didn't know whether you would admit a strange woman into your presence.

TIPU (*angry*): You've tricked me. You've inveigled the Padshah into giving you audience, into talking to you. Get out of here! Out!

(*The young visitor runs out. Tipu turns to the audience.*)

After consulting my closest advisers, I interpret this dream in the following fashion. May it please God, though these Marathas are dressed in male attire, they will in fact prove to be women.

(*The Maratha court in Pune. Nana Phadnavis, the Maratha states-man, with Charles Malet, representative of Lord Cornwallis.*)

MALET: Nana Sahib, Our Governor-General-in-Council, Lord Cornwallis, would like to reassure the Maratha court at Pune that we have no intention of entering into confronta-tion with any of the Indian princes. Our Board of Control in London has advised our Governor General explicitly to adopt a pacific and defensive system since we, the Honour-able East India Company, are completely satisfied with the possessions we already have.

NANA: That's good news! But then tell me, Malet Sahib, why are you here?

MALET: We wish to assure the Maratha rulers that we are good friends who can be relied upon in moments of crisis.

NANA: Ah! That raises two questions. First, is there a crisis?

MALET: That's for our friends to decide for themselves. The Com-pany recognizes, sir, your right to assess your own political situation. Article XVI of the Treaty of Versailles states—at the insistence of the English, I might add—that neither the French nor the English shall get involved in what we would consider differences of opinion between Indian princes.

NANA: Very kind of you. That leads us to the second question. Are we your friends?

MALET: Surely the great Nana Sahib is jesting. Need the question be asked?

NANA: Who *are* your friends?

MALET: Apart from your honourable court at Pune, sir, there's the Scindia, the other Maratha Chiefs, the Nizam of Hyderabad, the Nawabs of Carnatic and Oudh, the Rajahs of Travancore and Cochin.

NANA: A dreary lot. I can't stand Shinde or the Nizam and I mean to give them a good hiding soon. The others are beneath contempt.

MALET: In view of what I've already said we have nothing to say on that.

NANA: I see Tipu Sultan Khan Sahib of Mysore is conspicuously missing from your list.

MALET: As you know, Nana Sahib, we are having a little trouble with him.

NANA: I see. So signing a Treaty of Perpetual Peace with someone does not constitute a gesture of friendship for the English.

MALET: Oh, but it does. And I'm sorry if I gave the impression that it does not.

NANA: You signed a treaty of friendship with Tipu Sultan Khan Sahib not so long ago at Mangalore.

MALET: The Treaty of Mangalore was forced on us.

NANA (*warming up*): Treaties are always forced upon the losing side, Malet Saheb. I'm sorry, but your 'friends' are a bunch of nincompoops. Tipu is worth a hundred of the Nizam, who is nothing but a whining little limpet. I must accuse you English of duplicity—

MALET: Surely not, sir—

NANA: We Marathas too have signed a Treaty of Perpetual Peace with Tipu Sultan and we have more regard for our word than the English seem to have for theirs. I would prefer to deal with the *vakils* of Tipu Sultan who are waiting outside the door this minute. They at least do not take me for a brainless weather vane.

MALET: I urge you, sir, there's no cause for that feeling. The moment he arrived in India, Lord Cornwallis assured our Board of Control that we neither wish to indulge in a breach of the Treaty of Mangalore nor contravene the solemn injunction in Pitt's India Act—

NANA: Mis-sterr Malet, your mind swarms with documents. Please do not try to confuse me with conflicting quotations. I am a Brahmin. I am an expert at it.

MALET: May we then stick to facts, Your Honour?

NANA: That's better. Yes, the facts.

MALET: Of which there's only one that matters to us. Tipu has attacked the Rajah of Travancore, who as I said before, is one of our friends.

NANA: The Raja of Tiruvidankoor is a mischievous little rat who would have kept a respectful distance from Tipu Sultan had he not been certain that Cornwallis would support his antics.

MALET: We cannot watch while our friends are harassed.

NANA: Then you go ahead and fight Tipu Sultan. I have nothing against him.

MALET: Except for the vast Maratha territories which his father grabbed unjustly and which Tipu still retains.

(*Pause.*)

May we point out that when Tipu made his peace with the Marathas, he returned all his recent acquisitions but not his father's? While the bravery of the Marathas is known the world over, so, sir, is Tipu's. If the Marathas ever face Tipu alone, it's likely to be a stalemate again. If you'll permit a rash observation, sir, it's unlikely that you will subdue him enough to make him surrender those territories. I'm sorry but that's a fact which I'm sure the wise Nana Sahib will not deny.

NANA: Nor will Nana Sahib deny the infinite cunning of your stratagem. The world will see instantly that even the Marathas needed the help of the English?

MALET: Sir, Lord Cornwallis is aware that such a misapprehension may be created and is most anxious to prevent it. He therefore suggests that the Marathas, the Nizam and the Honourable Company declare war on Tipu independently of each other. There will be no open collaboration. We shall attack from three different directions—separately.

(*Pause.*)

The Marathas have been robbed. The Nizam has been robbed. The Rajah of Travancore has been attacked. To be honest, sir, we, the English, do not like his repeated attempts to join hands with the villainous French, though of course they are our friends after the recent treaty. The Governor General hopes that the Maratha Chief will use this opportunity to obtain reparation and recover the territories seized unjustly by Tipu Sultan's father, Haider Ali, and will join us in punishing a man who we believe is the enemy of all mankind.

(*Pause.*)

NANA (*thoughtful*): Uh hum!

(*The inner chamber of Tipu's palace. Tipu is sitting alone, next to Queen Ruqayya Banu's bed, watching, with an affectionate smile, the rumpus going on. Off-stage, we hear the almost life-like growls of a mechanical tiger and the equally life-like screams of a human doll. It all sounds real at the start. But soon peals of laughter from the children dispel any sense of real violence.*)

RUQAYYA BANU (*laughing off-stage*): What will they think of next!

MUIZ (*off-stage*): Shall I play it again?

RUQAYYA (*off-stage*): Enough now, Muizuddin. It's a dreadful toy.

MUIZ (*off-stage*): Just once, please.

TIPU: Let them. Why are you stopping them?

(*More growls and screams again along with the screams of relish from the princes. Ruqayya Banu enters and reclines on the bed. She is obviously not too well. Abdul Khaliq comes and sits, almost clinging to her. Muizuddin and Fath Haidar continue off-stage.*)

MUIZ: It's so real…terrifying!

FATH: I wish there was a little blood! That would have made it even more frightening.

RUQAYYA: Be quiet, Fath Haidar. Come here, both of you. The toy is violent enough as it is. I don't like it. Why do you bring such awful things for our children?

TIPU: At their age I had to deal with real blood and gore. You've brought them up to be too soft!

ABDUL KHALIQ: Mother, you've been laughing at it too.

TIPU: And how!

RUQAYYA: That's what I don't like. I wouldn't care to be present when a man is being mauled by a tiger. So why should I enjoy it when a toy tiger tears up a man? It's unnatural.

(*Fath Haidar and Muizuddin come in, excited.*)

FATH: But, Mother, the mechanism—it's so ingenious—so life-like—

TIPU: The French are just superb at that kind of thing.

FATH: Father, can't our craftsmen produce something like this?

TIPU: Actually I asked the toy-makers of Chennapatna before ordering it from the French. And do you know what they said? 'Oh sir, our ancient tradition is dedicated to things beautiful. Let the foreigners handle these cruel toys!'

(*Ruqayya Banu laughs along with Tipu.*)

Imagine their gall! I built that wretched village into a centre for glassware, musical instruments, and toys. And they give me a lecture on the morality of aesthetics.

RUQAYYA: Good for them. Truly, I wish there were more like them around you.

MUIZ: Father, that man being attacked by the tiger...he's an Englishman, isn't he?

TIPU: Yes, he is.

MUIZ: Is that because the French don't like the English?

TIPU: Yes, and I don't like them either.

RUQAYYA: And they don't like you.

TIPU: Fair enough. (*To the children*) But let me tell you, I've had two teachers in my life. My father, who taught me war, and the English, who taught me trade. They taught me that the era of the camel is over, that it is now the age of the sailing ship. And they dislike me for being so adept a pupil.

RUQAYYA: Why are they after you now?

TIPU: No idea. I actually asked the English Governor in Madras to send a delegation to Seringapatam so we could sort our differences out. But he declined. It would reduce them in the eyes of the other Indian princes!

RUQAYYA: You can hardly expect them to love a man who plays with a toy like that—

TIPU: The English have better reasons than that. I have refused to have their Resident at my court.

MUIZ: Can I play it again?

RUQAYYA: No, you can't. I want to lie down. I feel tired.

TIPU: Do, yes. Hasina, give her another pillow. Good. Fath Haidar, have the tiger removed to the Diwan-i-Aam, before your mother shoots it down.

FATH (*laughs*): Yes, Father.
(*Exits.*)

TIPU: Abdul Khaliq, can't you sit up like a prince? Your mother's trying to rest. You don't have to crawl into her bed every time—

RUQAYYA: Let him be. He's my baby.

TIPU: And he's remained one. Look at Muizuddin. He isn't cuddling up to you all the time. And he's younger.

RUQAYYA: Enough, please. You spend so little time with them. And then you are forever reprimanding them. Sit down, please. Relax. Be their father, not their Sarkar-e-Khudadad. Why do you drive yourself like this? Please, slow down a bit—

TIPU: This land is *ours* and it's rich, overflowing with goods the world hungers for, and we let foreigners come in and rob us of our wealth! Today the Indian princes are all comatose, wrapped in their opium dreams. But some day they'll wake up and throw out the Europeans. So the only way the Europeans can ensure their profits for all time to come is by becoming rulers themselves. You see? It's them or us. Now you rest. The hakims say you must take care of yourself and not get excited over trifles. There are enough people to look after palace chores...

RUQAYYA: They don't bother me. You know what worries me—You!

TIPU: I'll give the English and the Nizam a drubbing they'll remember till the end of time.

RUQAYYA: You're worried about the Marathas.

TIPU: Yes, I am. Only Mahadji Shinde understands the English. The Marathas of Pune are coy, flirtatious, unreliable. But I need their help, so I've made peace with them. So long as they keep out of this conflict—and I have returned the territories I had conquered from them—I've nothing to worry about.

HASINA (*enters*): May the Lord protect Your Majesty. The Honourable Mir Sadiq is here with our *vakils* from Pune.

TIPU (*aghast*): We talk of the Marathas and our *vakils* from Pune arrive! That doesn't portend well. May God's will be done. Take care of yourself, Ruqayya.

(*Exits.*)

MUIZ: I'm going with Father.

(*Exits.*)

HASINA: Madam, the whole palace is in turmoil—

RUQAYYA: What's it, Hasina?

HASINA: Our *vakils* have been driven out of Pune. The English have succeeded in their manipulation. The Marathas too have declared war on us.

ABDUL: Why, Mother—is it bad for *vakils* to come back?

RUQAYYA: Don't talk, child. I can barely breathe. May it please God it is not the disaster I fear it is.

(*Ruqayya gasps. Hasina anxiously calls out.*)

HASINA: Madam—Madam—

ABDUL: What's happened to Mother?

HASINA: Please wait here, Your Highness. I'll fetch the *hakim*. Please look after her.

(*Runs out. Kirmani and Mackenzie.*)

MACKENZIE: In 1790, Lord Cornwallis invaded Mysore. The Nizam and the Marathas launched parallel attacks. A see-saw war stretched over two years, with no end in sight. Cornwallis reached the foot of the fort of Seringapatam, saw the futility of trying to capture it and retreated disheartened. At one point in the campaign, he wrote to his friend, the Bishop of Lichfield:

CORNWALLIS (*entering*): My spirits are almost worn out and if I cannot soon overcome Tipu, I think the plagues and mortifications of this most difficult war will overcome me. (*Exits.*)

KIRMANI: But on their return journey, the English forces ran into the Marathas with their abundant supplies. The two joined forces and attacked Seringapatam. Tipu Sultan was forced to sue for peace.

Act Two

23 February 1792. The square in front of the big mosque in Serin-
gapatam, packed with senior citizens, generals, and courtiers. A
buzz of anxiety and suppressed excitement, which subsides when
Poornaiya stands up to speak.

POORNAIYA: Noblemen of the court, the Sarkar-e-Ahmadi has
   asked me to offer you his most contrite apologies for keeping
   you waiting. But the senior *hakim* is here with his advisers
   attending to the Queen. The Sultan will be here with you
   as soon as the hakims finish their examination.

A NOBLEMAN: Honourable Poornaiya, may we know the state of
   the Queen's health?

POORNAIYA: The Sultan wishes me to tell you that even the *hakims*
   do not know what the ailment is. The Queen, as you know,
   has been ill for a while now and has a fever that refuses to
   come under control.

NOBLEMAN 2: Could it be that the perils facing our state have
   affected her?

POORNAIYA: Almost certainly. The Queen loves us all like her
   children. She is also concerned about the Sultan's health.
   He is under enormous pressure as you know.

MIR SADIQ (*announces*): His Majesty!

CROWD: God save the King! God grant the Queen a long life!

TIPU: *Inshallah!* (God willing.)

CROWD: *Inshallah!*

(*A long pause.*)

TIPU: I crave your pardon for this delay. You are all noblemen, officers, generals, pillars on whom this kingdom of God rests. You know why I have invited you all here. The enemies hold our city in a python's embrace. The Honourable Ghulam Ali Khan has just returned from France. He knows how to deal with foreigners. I therefore sent him to negotiate with the enemy. It proved to be a most propitious choice. We have three enemies—the English, the Marathas, and the Nizam. But only the English spoke. The other two nodded in respectful silence.

(*Reactions from the crowd.*)

The Honourable Ghulam Ali Khan has returned with the terms of peace. I want your advice on how I should proceed next. We are gathered in front of our chief mosque. I place this Quran Shareef in front of you. With the Holy Book as my witness, I ask you to speak what your heart feels. Honourable Poornaiya, will you please read out the terms dictated by Lord Cornwallis?

POORNAIYA: There are four conditions in the main. One: all English prisoners taken by His Majesty as well as his father of hallowed memory, Haidar Ali, to be released, unconditionally.

TIPU: Let's hear the Honourable Ghulam Ali Khan on that.

GHULAM: Discussions of this condition were accompanied by much vituperation by the English. They said that we had ill-treated our English prisoners of war. We pointed out that we had treated them as we treat our own prisoners—despite much provocation. And then we pointed out that the English who had surrendered to us were at least alive as prisoners of war while our men who surrendered to the enemy—where were they? What happened to them? There was no answer.

(*Angry muttering from the crowd.*)

TIPU: Go on, Honourable Poornaiya.

POORNAIYA: Two: cession of half our domain, adjacent to the territories of the English, the Marathas, and the Nizam.
(*Angry reaction from the crowd.*)

CITIZEN 1: Why should we accept these humiliating terms, Your Majesty? Let's go on with the war—

CITIZEN 2: We'll fight to the last man rather than—
(*Tipu silences them by raising his hand.*)

TIPU: Qilledar Nadeem Khan, you are in charge of our fort. What do you say?

NADEEM (*after a slight hesitation*): If it was a question of facing only the English, we could take the initiative instantly. We could scatter them now as we did a few months ago. But the Marathas are supporting them.

MIR SADIQ: And the Nizam's troops joined them a week ago.

TIPU: We are blocked by our own people. I wrote to the Nizam: 'The benefits of unity and harmony among the followers of Islam are known to you. How can we increase the splendour of our Faith? I shall do as you guide me.'
(*Pause.*)

But we have been snubbed by the lack of even an acknowledgement of our letter. What is the state of the army's morale, Honourable Qamaruddin?

QAMARUDDIN: For two years we have fought and fought well. The soldiers are now tired. For weeks, they've been sleeping on their feet. I do not know how long they can hold out.

TIPU: Do you agree with that, Qilledar Sahib?

NADEEM: Yes, Your Majesty.

TIPU: So we have no alternative but to sue for peace?
(*Pause.*)

God's will be done. Please, do not expend your energies on these matters. Territories come and go. We fight, we gain, we lose. Proceed.

POORNAIYA: An indemnity of six crores.

GHULAM: At this point the English asked us to produce our revenue receipts. Our Chief Peshkar produced them. The English said they doubted the figures...

(*Reaction from the crowd.*)

TIPU: Silence, please! Let the Noble Ghulam Ali Khan complete his report.

GHULAM: We pointed out that if their own allies, the Marathas or the Nizam, had been asked for similar accounts, no such accounts would be forthcoming.

(*Pause.*)

For they have no such system.

(*Laughter from the audience.*)

TIPU: The pity of it is that the representatives of the Nizam and the Marathas were sitting there—swallowing all these jibes without a murmur.

(*Pause.*)

Proceed, Poornaiya.

(*Silence.*)

Poornaiya...

(*Pause.*)

Please!

POORNAIYA (*overcome*): I cannot, Your Majesty. I beg to be excused...

TIPU: All right then. I'll read it out myself. Hand me the paper. (*Reads.*) The last condition: two hostages to be handed over to the English to be kept with them until the terms of the treaty are duly fulfilled.

(*Pause.*)

Two of my sons.

(*Uproar. Angry protests.*)

CITIZEN 1: This is outrageous—

CITIZEN 2: If our soldiers hear of this, they'll rise to a man and fall on the English.

CITIZEN 3: Please, please, Your Majesty, do not accept this humiliation. We would rather die—

CITIZEN 4: This is barbaric.

TIPU: Noblemen, please, silence! I beg of you. Honourable Ghulam Ali Khan, recount to our noblemen what Lord Cornwallis said.

GHULAM: The English Lord in all kindness assured us that having only one son himself, he experienced the affection of a parent in more than an ordinary degree; but even his own child could not be received by him with greater tenderness than ours.

(*Pause.*)

TIPU: Instead of demanding two particular sons, he would accept any two of our sons. Whom can I send? Fath Haidar? Yes, he is the eldest. Old enough to be sent. Though he is dear to me, I would send him. But the English are a very proper nation. They will not accept him, for his mother was not my legal consort.

(*Reaction.*)

So that leaves—Abdul Khaliq, who is eight and Muizuddin, only a few months younger.

(*Reactions of horror, anger, revulsion. Then slow silence.*)

The other children are still at their nurses' breasts. Should I send my two little boys as hostages?

(*Shouts of 'No', 'Please don't accept—'*)

Shall I then accept the destruction of our city?

(*Pause.*)

That's the choice before us.

(*Long silence.*)

This is the new language that has come into our land: English.

This is the culture of that language: English. Boys of seven and eight as hostages of war.

CITIZEN: How can the city wish to remain safe while the lives of our princes are in danger?

TIPU: Danger? Yes. But what danger? Did you not hear what Lord Cornwallis says? The English will not harm our children. They'll not poison them or kill them, for there's no financial profit in it. What will the John Company gain in gold and silver and land by harming my sons? They'll not harm my children.

(*Pause. He is overcome.*)

The danger is: they'll teach my children their language, English. The language in which it is possible to think of children as hostages. All I can try to do is agree to their conditions and conclude the treaty in a hurry—before my children have learnt to think in those terms.

(*Pause.*)

So we accept their demands. Honourable Mir Sadiq, bring the seal. We shall affix our signature. There! Now my dear noblemen, my...

(*His voice cracks. A long pause. To Mir Sadiq*)

Will you please thank the noblemen for coming here and tell them that the meeting is adjourned? Suddenly I seem to have lost my voice.

MIR SADIQ (*in tears*): His Majesty wishes the noblemen to retire—
(*The crowd departs, also in tears. When Mir Sadiq, Poornaiya, Nadeem Khan, Ghulam Ali Khan, and Qamaruddin get up to take leave, Tipu gestures to them to sit down. They sit. There is a very long silence.*)

POORNAIYA: Your Majesty, how will the Queen take the news in her present condition? Will her health be able to bear the shock?

TIPU: God has been angry with us, Poornaiya. But He has not

let us down entirely. I was late for this meeting because—I had to bid goodbye to Begum Ruqayya Banu. She left us this morning.

POORNAIYA: God save us!

(*Exclamations of shock and distress from the others.*)

TIPU: I waited till she breathed her last. I am lucky. She died without knowing I had bartered her sons for my kingdom.

MIR SADIQ: But—Your Majesty—

TIPU: And I gave strict orders that there was to be no wailing or weeping till this meeting with the noblemen was over. I didn't want tears to blind the judgement of my advisers.

(*Wailing is heard in the background.*)

The dead are happy. They go. And I've seen too many dead to care about death anymore. It's my sons I have to worry about now. Poornaiya, send for the Chief Astrologer of the Chennapatna temple. Ask him to study the stars and set the most auspicious moment for the departure of my sons. Ghulam Ali Khan, will you accompany your nephews? I don't want my babies to feel their family abandoned them totally—although that's what it amounts to finally.

GHULAM ALI: I shall go with them, Your Majesty. I shall spend every moment with them until they are reunited with you.

TIPU (*getting excited*): Mir Sadiq, tell the British—tell them my sons must be received properly. With full honours. They are princes. There are to be no lapses. Not the smallest—(*Almost angry*) I shall not tolerate it.

MIR SADIQ: Of course, Your Majesty.

TIPU: And we'll send them out as heroes, symbols of the glory of their land. In full splendour. A splendour that'll put the foreigners to shame—and cover up my own sense of shame.

(*The inner chamber of the palace. Ghulam Ali Khan enters.*)

GHULAM ALI: Hasina—Hasina—

HASINA (*enters*): Sir—

GHULAM ALI: Hasina, call the princes Abdul Khaliq and Muizuddin here. Tell them I want to talk to them. Only them, mind you, no one else.

HASINA: Yes, sir.
(*Exits.*)

GHULAM (*murmuring to himself*): I pray to you, God, give me strength to face this moment. Make me strong.
(*Muizuddin, Abdul Khaliq, and Fath Haidar enter with Hasina.*)

CHILDREN (*in a subdued voice*): Our salutations, Uncle.

GHULAM: Oh, Fath Haidar! Er—

HASINA: Sir, what could I do? I said you only wanted to meet—

GHULAM: All right. All right. Leave us now.
(*Hasina withdraws. Pause.*)
Children, there are times when God tests us—to see how strong we are—whether we truly believe in His Will. This is such a time.

ABDUL KHALIQ (*embraces him*): I want to go to Mother—I want Mother—please—

GHULAM: Listen, princes. God has called your mother away. We must not cry about that. We must not question His Will. You have borne that test like princes. There's another test ahead of us now and I want you to face it equally bravely.

FATH: Yes, Uncle.
(*Ghulam Ali pointedly addresses his remarks to the two younger children which is difficult to do without snubbing Fath Haidar.*)

GHULAM: The English have suggested that the two of you visit them and stay with them—as guests. For how long we don't know, but it won't be for too long. Of course, I'll be there with you all the time.

FATH: I am ready, Uncle. And I don't need anyone with me. I'm old enough to go on my own.

(*Pause.*)

GHULAM: I'm sorry, Fath Haidar. The English want only...heirs to the throne.

FATH: Oh, I'm sorry. I'm sorry I offered myself.

GHULAM: No, no, no. Don't take it to heart, son. Your father loves you. We all love you. You, Muizuddin, Abdul Khaliq, you're all the same to us. But this is politics.

FATH: I understand, Uncle. I'm sorry I spoke out of turn.

GHULAM (*helpless*): I'm afraid it has to be Muizuddin and Abdul Khaliq. (*To them*) You see how Fath Haidar volunteered without hesitation? Are you willing to come with me, children?

MUIZ: I'm scared, Uncle. But I will go with you.

GHULAM: That's a good boy. And you, Abdul Khaliq?

(*No answer.*)

I'm sure you are ready too.

ABDUL (*tearful*): I don't want to go, Uncle...I'm frightened...

FATH: He's been listening to all kinds of stupid rumours.

GHULAM: There's nothing to be afraid of. And I'll be there.

ABDUL: I don't want to go.

GHULAM: Look...

ABDUL (*whimpering*): Please, don't make me—Please—

GHULAM: Now, now, Abdul. You are eight years old. A man already! You saw that Fath Haidar volunteered instantly. So did Muizuddin and he's younger than you.

ABDUL: I want Mother—

FATH (*viciously*): Cry-baby. Always a cry-baby!

GHULAM: Please, Fath Haidar, let's be calm...

ABDUL: I want Mother. She wouldn't have let me go—She wouldn't have sent me—

GHULAM: Abdul Khaliq, God has left us no choice. He has taken your mother to his bosom. And you have to go to the English for a few months only. Now, your father will be here any moment. He is already shattered—by everything, but more at the thought of losing you. You have to give him courage. Will you?

HASINA (*enters*): Sir, the Master is here.

GHULAM (*almost panic-stricken*): I told you God is testing us. The test doesn't begin when you face the English. They are our sworn enemies. I'm sure you'll know how to face them. The test is now! Let's see how you pass it.

(*Tipu enters, in a daze.*)

Greetings, Your Majesty.

(*Pause.*)

Your Majesty, I've talked to the princes. They await your orders.

(*Long silence. Tipu stands staring.*)

Your Majesty—

(*Silence. Gently,*)

Prince Muizuddin—

MUIZ: Father, I'm ready to go to the English.

(*Pause.*)

ABDUL: I am too, Father.

TIPU: Oh God!

(*Music. Cheering. Celebrations. A salute of guns. Diwan-i-Aam. Tipu with Kirmani, Poornaiya and Mir Sadiq.*)

TIPU: Then? Then what happened?

KIRMANI: The procession led by camel *harakāras* and standard bearers—followed by a hundred lancers with spears inlaid with silver—entered the English camp. Then came the princes on caparisoned elephants.

TIPU: How beautiful they looked, the two angels! In white muslin robes and pearls and turbans. Ruqayya Banu, you were too much of a queen to stay behind to witness my shame. Still I wish you were here. You would have been proud of them—as the whole city was.

KIRMANI: They were followed by the escort guard of the infantry and cavalry—

TIPU (*impatient*): I know. I know. Janaab Kirmani, I saw all that from the ramparts. Tell me what happened in the English camp.

KIRMANI: The English seemed stunned by our magnificence. The princes were received with a twenty-one-gun salute.

TIPU: Yes, yes, we heard that. That was good. That was proper—

KIRMANI: A battalion of Bengal Sepoys formed a guard of honour as the princes moved down the English lines. Arms were presented, drums were beaten.

TIPU: Excellent! Excellent!

KIRMANI: Lord Cornwallis and his officers received the princes at the entrance of his tent. He took each prince by hand and sat them down on the right and left of his chair—

TIPU: And my children—were they scared? Did they appear nervous?

KIRMANI: No, Your Majesty, not a whit.

TIPU: What about Abdul Khaliq? He was always a little unsure of himself.

KIRMANI: Your Majesty, the dignity of their bearing and their self-possession drew praise from every Englishman. Then the Honourable Ghulam Ali Khan said to Lord Cornwallis: 'These children were this morning the sons of the Sultan, my master. Their situation is now changed and they must look up to Your Lordship as their Father.'

TIPU: Oh God! God! Why didn't I die before I heard these words?

Ruqayya Banu, why didn't you take me with you? How did
I come to this?

KIRMANI: Lord Cornwallis assured our Ambassador that the
children would not feel the loss of a father's care—

TIPU: He must have known these words would reach me and
pull out my entrails—

KIRMANI: —and that his protection was fully extended to
them. The princes smiled at that. There was applause. The
princes presented Lord Cornwallis with the Persian sword.
He inspected it and praised its craftsmanship. And then he
gave each prince a gold watch.

TIPU: And what did my children do with the watches?

KIRMANI: They hardly looked at them. They passed them on to
the attendants with barely a glance.

TIPU: That's it! That's it! They're well brought up, my sons.

KIRMANI: Then the *attar* of roses and betel leaves were distributed
and the princes returned to their tents of fine chintz. And
Your Majesty must listen to this. As soon as they were inside
the tent—

(*Laughs.*)

TIPU: Yes? Why do you laugh?

KIRMANI: As soon as they were inside the tent, the princes asked for
the watches and started busily examining their mechanisms.

(*General laughter.*)

TIPU: They're my sons, after all! My darling princes! Nadeem
Khan, fire a salute to the English from the fort tomorrow
morning. Let them know we appreciate the way they have
received my sons. And Poornaiya, send the English a crore
and a half as the first instalment of our payment.

POORNAIYA: Yes, Your Majesty.

TIPU: And Mir Sadiq, send word to the Marathas. I want to visit
their camp and see their Commander-in-Chief, Hari Pant
Phadke, before they depart.

MIR SADIQ: Is that wise, Your Majesty?

TIPU: Please do as I say. Now goodbye, gentlemen. Thank you.
I must retire.

ALL: May God protect the Sultan.

(*They withdraw. Tipu moves to his bed chamber. Sees the mattress
spread out on the bed.*)

TIPU: Chamberlain—

CHAMBERLAIN: Your Majesty—

TIPU: Remove the bed from my bed chamber. While my sons are
in foreign hands, I shall sleep on the bare stone floor.

(*Tipu undresses, sits on the stone floor. He takes out a string of
beads and starts reciting a Sufi Zikr—incantation—to himself. He
begins to sway as in a trance. He sways more and more violently
as the lights darken. A voice calls out to him softly in the dark.*)

VOICE: Tipu—Tipu—

TIPU: Who's that? Is that you, Father?

HAIDAR: Yes, it's me. Haidar.

(*Lights come on slowly to reveal a spectral landscape. Tipu looks
around frantically.*)

TIPU: Where are you, Father?

HAIDAR: Here, under this tree.

TIPU: Under this—? Father, why are you lying there? What's
happened to you?

HAIDAR: I'm maimed, Tipu. I have no limbs.

TIPU: But you never lost any limb.

HAIDAR: You have maimed me, Tipu. You have cut off my limbs
and handed them over to the enemy.

TIPU (*low*): Yes, Father. I've done that. Have you come to pun-
ish me?

HAIDAR: What punishment would be adequate, do you think?

TIPU: I don't know, Father. You remember, once I messed up your
campaign and you gave me a lashing, almost skinned me

alive. My body still bears those welts—such scars that I'm ashamed to undress in front of anyone. This crime is much worse than that.

HAIDAR: I can't do that now. I have no arms.

TIPU: Shall I lash myself for you?
(*He starts whipping himself.*)

HAIDAR: No melodrama, I pray you. No hysterics. Please. You've gone soft. You spend too much time with your account books.

TIPU: You spent your life on horseback—making conquests. I have to consolidate your gains. That can't be done on horseback. The English are stronger now.

HAIDAR: And whose fault is it?

TIPU: I hate them—and they return the compliment.

HAIDAR: Then why did you let Cornwallis escape? (*No answer.*) When he was retreating from Seringapatam in shame and desperation, your Amirs and Khans begged you to attack. You stood on the ramparts and did nothing.

TIPU: I was paralysed.

HAIDAR: You let Cornwallis go.

TIPU: You would have made mincemeat of him, I know. But I vacillated.

HAIDAR: You're scared of them.

TIPU: No, I'm not. If I were scared, I would have ordered a slaughter. But, Father, often, suddenly, I see myself in them—I see these white skins swarming all over the land and I wonder what makes them so relentless? Desperate? Most of them are no older than Fath Haidar. What drives these young lads to such distant lands through fever, dysentery, alcohol so—often to death—wave after wave? They don't give up. Nor would I. Sometimes I feel more confident of them than my own people. What makes them so unsparing towards themselves? Is it only money?

HAIDAR: You're beginning to think like a trader.

TIPU (*angry*): No, if it was only for money, they would betray each other. But there's never any treachery against their own kind, no back-stabbing. They believe in the destiny of their race. Why can't we?

(*Pause.*)

When our fort was besieged by Cornwallis, I knew several of my officers had already started secret negotiations with him. I even knew who they were. My trusted officers. Yet I couldn't expose them without bringing the whole edifice down. I had to keep saying they were the true pillars of my kingdom, that I depended on their loyalty to me and my family—and hope for the best. Hope that when the moment came, they wouldn't stab me in the back. But the English fight for something called England. What is it? It's not a religion that sustains them, nor a land that feeds them. They wouldn't be here if it did. It's just a dream, for which they are willing to kill and die. Children of England! They have conquered our land, plundered its riches. And now they've started taking away our children. Mine—

(*Haidar laughs.*)

I will not let them. Father, I'll restore your limbs. Father, where are you? Father—Father—Come back—

(*Darkness swallows them up. When lights come on we are in the Maratha camp. Hari Pant Phadke is waiting for Tipu Sultan.*)

HARI PANT: Welcome, Tipu Sultan Khan Saheb. Welcome to the Maratha camp. This is a most pleasant surprise—

TIPU: It's a custom in our land to bid goodbye to guests personally before they leave.

HARI PANT: Even when the guest was unwelcome?

TIPU: I did not make you unwelcome. We met last seven years ago and we parted as friends. We swore there would be everlasting

peace between us. I still do not know what changed the
situation. But I mustn't be impolite to my guest. I hope your
family is well.

HARI PANT: Yes, thank you. And yours?

(*An embarrassed pause as Hari Pant realizes his faux pas.*)

I want to assure you, Khan Sahib, that we Marathas were
not party to that deal—about taking your children hostage.
We are extremely disturbed by it.

TIPU: You were 'not party'. What does that mean, Hari Pant?
You disagreed with it?

HARI PANT: Yes, we did.

TIPU: And you were overruled?

HARI PANT: The Nizam stood by the English. We Marathas were
outvoted.

TIPU: Hari Pant, the English were fleeing in despair—I had
driven them back—when you came to their aid at Melukote.
Without your enormous bazaar of supplies, half their army
would have been wiped out, and the other half stumbling
towards Madras by now. You are the true victors of this war.
Yet you let the English dictate the terms!

HARI PANT: The English are our allies. After all, you have the French
working for you. You have sought French friendship.

TIPU: Friendship, yes! Working for me! Not dictating to me. You
have seen the new demands made by the English? I've just
received them.

HARI PANT (*evasive*): I've had no occasion to doubt the integrity
of the English. Cornwallis deals firmly but fairly.

TIPU: I am to cede half my kingdom adjacent to your territories—

HARI PANT: I know that. That was part of the initial agreement
between us.

TIPU: And you know what part of my lands they are demanding?
The province of Kodagu.

(*Pause.*)

You're silent. To which possession of the English is Kodagu adjacent? Will you tell Cornwallis that this wasn't the geography you had in mind when you discussed the terms of the treaty? You won't. For this is a convenient geography of his own invention, and you go along.

HARI PANT: Cornwallis has been honest with us. That's what counts. We have a third share of our joint conquests—

TIPU (*hoots with laughter*): You have what? Hari Pant, how can you say that without blushing? The share that you've been given is what my father had won from you Marathas forty years ago. What you've got is only a restitution of your earlier possessions. And in return you have given the English new territories: Salem, Dindigul, the Malabar coast with its coconuts and pepper and its magnificent ports. You are back where you were while the English now have the entire coastline of India. And remember, they are a sea-faring power. Mine is a landlocked kingdom, so I thirst for the sea, for today the sea is the key to power, to prosperity. You have the whole of the western coast. And instead of keeping the English out, you've permitted the shark into your waters and are trying to swim along with it.

HARI PANT: We only want what's ours—

TIPU: And how long will it remain yours? Where's the Raja of Tiruvidankoor in whose honour the English mounted this campaign? Thrown on the dung heap.

HARI PANT (*lamely*): He is no concern of ours.

TIPU: I would have torn this treaty and flung it in your faces and died in the breach sooner than consent to the cession of Kodagu. But they have my children! My sons! I asked for time to consider these preposterous terms and you know what their response has been? Instead of returning my children and continuing the battle, they have taken away their Mysore escort—and imprisoned my sons! Made them prisoners of war! How does that strike you, brave leader of the Marathas? Prisoners of war, aged seven and eight! So I'll capitulate—I'll give them what they want. Goodbye, Hari Pant. You are a wise man. And I hope you have given thought to why, when the English could have decimated me, they have left me with my kingdom.

HARI PANT: Khan Saheb, we insisted that your status was not to be touched—

TIPU: Rubbish. Cornwallis has saved me because without me in south India, you Marathas would become too powerful. You are being carefully contained. No, don't reply. And please don't come out of the tent to see me off. I shall find my way. This is still my land. Only one word of caution, Hari Pant. Make sure it's not your children next time.

(*Walks out.*)

(*Mackenzie and Kirmani.*)

MACKENZIE: The defeat of Tipu was a personal triumph for Lord Cornwallis. The stigma of York Town was washed off. The Crown conferred on him the title of 'Marquis'. In a fit of absent-mindedness, the Parliament forgot all about Pitt's India Act.

KIRMANI: It was two years before Tipu's sons were restored to him. When they were reunited, the boys laid their heads on their father's feet and he, leaning forward, touched them on their necks. No words were spoken.

MACKENZIE: Lord Cornwallis was succeeded by Sir John Shore as the Governor General. Seven years of peace ensued. And then came Richard Wellesley, Second Earl of Mornington—an ambitious young man of thirty-eight.

(*1798. Calcutta. Richard Wellesley, Earl of Mornington, the Governor General of India, with his younger brother Arthur Wellesley, a junior colonel in the Indian army and Colonel William Kirkpatrick.*)

MORNINGTON: Before my departure for India, the Board of Control made it clear to me that the East India Company was not to acquire any more territory in India. The Prime Minister, Mr Pitt, was emphatic on that score.

KIRK: Yes, Your Lordship.

MORNINGTON: I've been on the Board myself for the last four years and have had time to reflect on what would be the best course of action for us to take.

KIRK: Yes, Your Lordship.

MORNINGTON: It seems to me self-evident that we have to liquidate Tipu.

(*Kirkpatrick looks up startled, then turns to gauge Arthur Wellesley's reaction. Arthur is impassive.*)

KIRK: But, Your Lordship, Sir John—

MORNINGTON: My saintly predecessor was an evangelical Christian. If you kicked him on his right buttock, he would probably turn his left. He didn't know how to take offence.

WELLESLEY (*laughs*): I gather he preferred Jortin's Sermons to official dispatches.

MORNINGTON: He should have taken offence when Tipu sent a delegation to Napoleon inviting him to invade India. This flirtation with our enemy should not have been tolerated.

KIRK: But now, after the Battle of Nile, that's surely not a cause for concern.

MORNINGTON: In fact, Tipu should have been got rid of after the last Mysore war by Cornwallis. But he didn't. And since then Tipu has grown in power and prestige, which is more than can be said of our dear effete allies. We must hold Cornwallis guilty of grave lapse of judgement and Sir John of deliberate connivance. It's my duty as the new Governor General of India to set things right.

KIRK: Do you think Tipu will want to create trouble, Your Lordship? Madras doesn't think so.

MORNINGTON: Tipu is building a trading empire on the European model and succeeding eminently. We have driven the French and Dutch out of India, contained the Portuguese. Is there any reason why we should tolerate an upstart native? The longer the peace, the stronger will Tipu become.

KIRK: But, Your Lordship, Madras is opposed to any move against Tipu—

MORNINGTON: Kirkpatrick, I will not allow a bunch of incompetent hacks, cowering in fear, to arrogate to themselves the power of governing the empire committed to my care. I'll not let them thwart me. Make that absolutely clear to Madras.

KIRK: Yes, Your Lordship.

MORNINGTON: Good. Now let's start at the beginning and ponder the opening move. Has Tipu had anything to do with the French recently?

(Pause. Kirkpatrick doesn't know what to say.)
No dealings with Pondicherry? Chandernagore?

WELLESLEY: What about Mauritius? More romantic, I'd say. Strategically located. The right scale.

MORNINGTON: Anything there?

KIRK: We have information that some forty Frenchmen from Mauritius came to Mysore last year in search of employment—

MORNINGTON: They did? Excellent. So Tipu sends a secret mission to the French Governor of Mauritius. What's his name?

KIRK (Scottish pronunciation): Malarctic, sir.

MORNINGTON: Quite! (French pronunciation.) Malarctic—asking for a dispatch of ten thousand French and twenty thousand African troops. And Malarctic puts up a proclamation asking for volunteers—

KIRK (guarded): Not if the mission were secret, surely?
(Wellesley smiles.)

MORNINGTON: No need for subtlety. Let's take the shortest route.

One of our newspapers in Calcutta gets hold of a copy and publishes it—

KIRK: I shall contact a local editor, Your Lordship—

WELLESLEY: Is that necessary? I'm sure the Board of Control will accept Richard's word for it.

(*Kirkpatrick is suitably snubbed.*)

MORNINGTON: Of course, we shan't believe the report initially. We want Tipu's friendship. It gives us time to prepare.

KIRK: But won't Tipu deny such an allegation, Your Lordship?

(*Long silence.*)

I'm sorry, but protocol would seem to demand we give him an opportunity to recant or make amends or at least explain himself.

MORNINGTON: Tipu has had peaceful relations with us for the last seven years, which means he will not expect us to declare war. He is not in a state of preparedness. In fact, he's quite likely to be absorbed in silkworms and sandalwood forests. Shall we then give him adequate warning, William, and face a long-drawn-out, costly war?

WELLESLEY: We know the speed with which he can mobilize.

KIRK (*cowed*): I understand.

MORNINGTON: I shall of course write to Tipu seeking an explanation. But General Harris will despatch the letter only after he and General Stuart have entered the Mysore territory. Tell the Nizam and the Marathas we shall expect their presence, though it scarcely matters either way. As for our Governor in Madras, he gets confused by long messages. So keep our instructions to him brief: Tipu must go.

KIRK: Yes, Your Lordship.

(*Pause.*)

Would that be all?

MORNINGTON: Yes, thank you.

(*Kirkpatrick leaves.*)

WELLESLEY: I'm rearing to leave for Seringapatam.

MORNINGTON: You should indeed.

(*Pause.*)

Baird is keen to lead the assault against Tipu. He has been a prisoner of Tipu's and is eager to avenge himself.

WELLESLEY: I know.

MORNINGTON: I told him it wasn't done to take things so personally. But well, you know Baird. The Scotch temper. And then, perhaps it's just as well. He'll lead the assault. You will command the reserve—

WELLESLEY (*jumping up*): Oh, no, Richard, for goodness' sake. Not the reserve.

MORNINGTON: I know you are keen to prove yourself on the battlefield, but I don't need soldiers at the moment. I have an entire army at my command to throw against Tipu. I want you alive...to take command of Seringapatam after the battle.

WELLESLEY (*horrified*): You can't be serious.

MORNINGTON: You know I'm never not serious. I shall need someone there whom I can trust.

WELLESLEY: But, Richard, the Governor General of India appointing his own brother—

MORNINGTON: And a junior colonel at that! Quite right! Nothing's more reprehensible than nepotism that's half-hearted.

WELLESLEY: Listen, I'd rather—

MORNINGTON: I know what you'd rather. Look, Cornwallis still lumbers across our landscape, a senile rhinoceros, all decked up in finery. This man, who lost us our American colonies, can still 'lumber' because he defeated Tipu!

(*Pause.*)

I shall destroy Tipu. I shall decimate Seringapatam, within six months. If that's not merit, I don't know what public service is. Surely, it would entitle me to the same rank as Cornwallis. Arthur, the eyes of the world will be focussed on Seringapatam and I want my brother there—at the centre. The Commandant of the Fortress! After that, it's up to you.

WELLESLEY (*lamely*): But, Richard, the scandal—

MORNINGTON: Would you rather…crawl up?

(*Diwan-i-Aam. Tipu with Mir Sadiq, Poornaiya, Qamaruddin and Nadeem Khan.*)

TIPU: And now they have asked for four of my sons as hostages. And half my kingdom again—half of the half they left me last time.

(*Pause.*)

By the time the next Governor General takes over, I'll be left with half a street and none of my sons.

(*Pause.*)

Shall I accept?

(*Pause.*)

And don't say, Poornaiya, that you had warned me. I knew the English wouldn't like my extending my hand to the French. So what? Shall I spend the rest of my life looking with anxiety at the English for smiles of approval or frowns of displeasure? Today I am the only one in India who won't bow and scrape before them. So they want to crush me. I'm told England is buzzing with stories of what a monster I am and how I need to be chastised.

(*Pause.*)

Shall I allow myself to be chastised?

(*Pause.*)

The English make impossible conditions. They expect me to reject them. I could throw their whole strategy into confusion by accepting these terms. Shall I be subtle and accept?

MIR SADIQ: No, Your Majesty, we'll fight the English to the bitter end.

POORNAIYA: When your father picked me up, I was a mere clerk in a small god-forsaken town. I am what I am today because of the kindness of your family. No, Your Majesty, we will not yield. We'll fight the English to the last drop of our blood.

TIPU: What do you say, Nadeem Khan?

NADEEM: They have tricked us by declaring war at the last minute. But Seringapatam is impregnable. While I am in charge of the fort, Your Majesty may rest assured the English have no hope of winning.

TIPU: Thank you. Thank you all. That's what I wanted to hear. That's why I haven't called a general meeting like I did last time. I only wanted to know what you all felt. You know I am entirely dependent on your loyalty to me and my family.

MIR SADIQ: Who do we have but you, Sarkar?

TIPU: Your word is enough for me. If you will all stand behind me as one—

QAMARUDDIN AND POORNAIYA: We will, sir, we will.

TIPU (laughing): Then the future is ours.

VOICES: Inshallah! (God willing.)

POORNAIYA: Your Majesty, the Seer of the Monastery at Sringeri has conveyed his support to you.

TIPU: We are indeed fortunate.

POORNAIYA: Remembering that you gave them shelter when the Marathas sacked the monastery, the Swami has assured you of Goddess Sharada's blessings.

TIPU: We are protected by such blessings.

(Long silence. No one knows what to say. To a servant)

Incidentally, why is Bahadur Khan quiet today? Is he all right?

SERVANT: Yes, Sarkar. And resting.

TIPU (*fidgety*): Not even a growl?

(*Gets up.*)

Well then. Let's get ready. The meeting is adjourned.

(*They exit. The stage darkens.*)

KIRMANI: The English surrounded the fort of Seringapatam. On 4th May 1799, dawn broke on its ramparts.

(*Tipu's bedroom. Knocking on the door. Tipu enters tying his sword belt.*)

TIPU: Who is it?

FATH (*from outside*): Good morning, Father, it's me, Fath Haidar. Are you ready?

(*Tipu opens the door and lets his son in.*)

TIPU (*laughs*): Well, you are in a hurry, aren't you?

FATH: Of course I am. Qamaruddin, the Commander-in-Chief has sent word that our forces are assembled and rearing to attack.

TIPU: Good. Good! You know, Fath Haidar, I was a year younger than you when I first rode into battle with my father?

FATH: I was ready a long time ago.

TIPU: I know, I know, it's hard to accept that one's children grow up. You'll see for yourself.

POORNAIYA (*entering*): May God bring victory to Your Majesty.

TIPU: Good morning, Poornaiya. What news?

POORNAIYA: I have just been to see the Chief Astrologer of the Ranganatha Temple—

TIPU: And?

POORNAIYA: He says the stars have never been more propitious. Victory will be ours. The nine planets have been placated and offerings made to the guardians of the eight directions.

TIPU: Thank you, friend. One must pacify the stars. But when you and Mir Sadiq are around, I have little to fear. We must first check on our new French cannons.

POORNAIYA: I just ran into the officer in charge of the battery. He says the cannons are accurate and have an extraordinary range. We'll blow the British attack to smithereens.

MIR SADIQ (*enters, excited*): Your Majesty, Your Majesty, incredible news. I'm so excited I don't know where to start. The heavens are smiling on us.

TIPU: The Lord be praised! What is it, Mir Sadiq?

MIR SADIQ: The Nizam has sent this despatch—I'll read it out—

TIPU: Just tell me in a few words. We have no time to waste.

MIR SADIQ: The Nizam says he has at last seen his folly in backing the English. He's seen through their game. If Your Majesty loses, the next target will be the Nizam.

TIPU: Of course, I've been trying to drum that into that moron for the last sixteen years. Still, it's good he's woken up—

MIR SADIQ: The Marathas too have decided to throw in their lot with us.

TIPU: You're sure I am not dreaming all this!

MIR SADIQ: Here's the Qilledar, Nadeem Khan. What news, Nadeem Khan?

NADEEM: News only of God's smile, Your Majesty. Hari Pant Phadke is here, awaiting your audience. Shall I admit him?

QAMARUDDIN (*entering*): Your Majesty—

TIPU (*angry*): Yes, Commander-in-Chief? But you should not be here. You should—

QAMARUDDIN: Sir, I've just seen with my eyes a sight even my grandchildren will narrate with pride!

TIPU: What is it? Get to the point!

QAMARUDDIN: The English are withdrawing. They're in total disarray. Total confusion rules the ranks of the foreigners. I saw English generals squabbling like women in the market—

(*Cheers from those present.*)

HUBBUB: Congratulations, sir. God be praised! We have done it.

FATH: Let's attack them, Father. Let's not allow the English to get away this time—

TIPU: You speak like your grandfather. He was always one for aggressive tactics.

FATH: So shall we fall on them?

TIPU: Not today. Today we celebrate. We pray and thank God. With the Marathas and the Nizam on our side, we can chase the English into the sea any day.

(*Laughter.*)

Thank you, all. Together we have driven the English back—

POORNAIYA: We did nothing, sir. It's the way Your Majesty led all of us. The vision of the future you gave us.

ABDUL KHALIQ (*entering*): Father, Mother says the rose bush sent to you by the King of Pegu has blossomed. She says you must come and see it.

TIPU: Muizuddin, Fath Haidar, Abdul Khaliq, call the entire zenana out. Invite them to the ramparts to see the white plague depart. Let's all watch a new era dawn. Then we'll go to the garden and see the Pegu roses bloom.

ALL: Long live the Sultan! Allah be praised! Victory to the Sultan!

(*Cheers. They all depart. Music builds up to a crescendo and suddenly stops. A long silence.*)

KIRMANI: That was Tipu's last dream.

That afternoon he was killed in battle.

Mir Sadiq's conduct of the war was so openly treacherous that his own troops lynched him. Nadeem Khan, the Qilledar, had ordered a pay parade for his troops at the very moment of British assault, thus taking them away from the battlefront. Poornaiya slipped with alacrity into the post of Prime Minister under the new regime. Qamaruddin was by his side.

The battle of Seringapatam was lost before it had begun.

(*Roar of tigers in the background followed by gunfire and then silence.*)

MACKENZIE: The tigers of the palace were shot dead while the mechanical tiger was shipped off to London.

(*Richard Wellesley enters, followed by Arthur.*)

Richard Wellesley, Earl of Mornington, Governor General of the British possessions in the East Indies said in a letter to the Board of Directors of the Honourable East India company:

MORNINGTON: While the dreadful fate of the fallen ruler could not be contemplated without pain and regret, it should show the Indian princes the danger of inviting foreign invasion—against the British power.

MACKENZIE: Arthur Wellesley, the Commandant of Seringapatam, was launched on a spectacular career which culminated in his becoming the Duke of Wellington, the Conqueror of Napoleon, Prime Minister of England.

(*Richard congratulates Arthur. They exit entirely pleased with themselves.*)

Tipu Sultan's sons were moved out of Seringapatam and ended up in Calcutta, where they could be kept under surveillance.

(*Pause.*)

Within twenty years, the British had annexed the Maratha empire.

KIRMANI: It was not Tipu's dreams but his predictions that came true.

(*Pause.*)

Postscript. When India became independent in 1947, the families of maharajas who had bowed and scraped before the British masters were granted sumptuous privy purses by the Government of India while the descendants of Tipu Sultan were left to rot in the slums of Calcutta.

BALI: The Sacrifice

PREFACE

It is a tribute to the astuteness and sensitivity of Mahatma Gandhi that he saw so clearly the importance of non-violence to the cultural and political survival of India. Violence has been the central topic of debate in the history of Indian civilization. Vedic fire sacrifices, conducted by Brahmin priests, involved the slaughter of animals as offerings to the gods, which the Jains found repugnant. To the Jain, indulging in any kind of violence, however minor or accidental, meant forfeiting one's moral status as a human being. Later, the Buddhists too joined the debate, arguing for non-violence, but from their own philosophical standpoint.

The dialectic found some resolution when the Brahmins renounced blood sacrifice. Miniature figurines, made of dough, were substituted for live animals, a practice that continues to this day. Still, the Jains argued that this was no solution. Although no animals were slaughtered and no meat consumed, these figures of dough, mimicking the forms of real animals, clearly carried the original violent impulse within them. And why dough rather than, say, mud or chalk? Because an offering makes sense only if it is meant as food for gods and is, therefore, cooked and consumed by the devotees. Thus the priests had merely replaced actual violence with violence in intention, which, said the Jains, was no less dehumanizing. This argument gave the debate a much more complex ethical twist. The Jain position raises the question: if intended violence condemns one as surely as actual violence, that is, if one is morally responsible for merely intending to commit an act one has not actually carried out in real life, is one not shutting oneself up in a solipsistic world, a bleak, guilt-ridden existence with no hope of absolution?

For *Bali: The Sacrifice*, I have drawn upon the thirteenth-century Kannada epic, *Yashodhara Charite*, by Janna, which in turn refers back through an eleventh-century Sanskrit epic by Vadiraja to the ninth-century Sanskrit epic, *Yashastilaka*, by Somadeva Suri. Some elements of the tale have been traced back to the first century. Stories and legends play multiple roles in Indian culture. As the late Professor Bimal Krishna Matilal of All Souls, Oxford, has pointed out: 'Great epics, apart from being the source of everything else, constitute an important component of what we may term as moral philosophical thinking of the Indian tradition. ... Professional philosophers of India over the last two thousand years ... have very seldom discussed what we call moral philosophy today. ... The tradition itself was very self-conscious about moral values, moral conflicts and dilemmas, as well as difficulties of what we call practical reason or practical wisdom. This consciousness found its expression in the epic stories and narrative literature.' *(Moral Dilemmas in the Mahabharata*, Shimla and New Delhi, 1989).

I first came across the myth of the Cock of Dough when I was still in my teens. Since then, my career as playwright has been littered with discarded drafts of dramatized versions of it. But looking back, I am happy closure eluded me, for the myth continued to reveal unexpected meanings with passing years. Though many of these versions were presented on stage, helping me to come to terms with the tale, I must remember with gratitude an early production, in Hindi, by Satyadev Dubey, featuring Naseeruddin Shah, Ratna Pathak Shah, Sunila Pradhan and Satyadev himself.

I rewrote the play from scratch, not for the first time, when the Leicester Haymarket Theatre commissioned me to write for them. My grateful thanks are due to Vayu Naidu, the Commissioning Producer, and Nona Shepphard, the director, who also worked closely with me on the text as dramaturges. Happily, Naseeruddin and Ratna again agreed to act in the play, but as the Mahout and the Queen Mother rather than as the royal couple. During the two years it took to bring the play to the stage, Naseeruddin acted in the film, *Monsoon Wedding*, and made himself internationally famous. Sometimes the stars are on your side.

Finally, I must acknowledge the kindness of Neelum Singh, who has retyped innumerable drafts and put up cheerfully with my niggling alterations.

London   GIRISH KARNAD

Bali: The Sacrifice was first presented at the Haymarket Theatre, Leicester, on 31 May 2002. The cast was as follows:

NASEERUDDIN SHAH	The Mahout
NEVE TAYLOR	The Queen
GARY TURNER	The King
RATNA PATHAK SHAH	The Queen Mother
Directed by	NONA SHEPPHARD
Designed by	MARSHA RODDY
Music by	ANDREW DODGE
Commissioning Producer	VAYU NAIDU

QUEEN: As the world is divided
         into two orbs:
         one lit up by the sun
         the other hid in the shade,
         so also the human soul,
         the habitation of gods,
         is split into two realms—
         one of the spirits that adore
         the blood and gore
         of the bright, shining blade
         slicing smoothly
         through the lamb
         and the other
         ruled by the spirits that bid
         you pause
         before you use
         the knife on a sapling
         or clap in the air—
         lest you harm a life.

Lights brighten to reveal the whole stage:
The inner sanctum of a ruined temple.
The pedestal on which the deity once stood is still intact. But as for
the image, only the feet survive, suggesting a standing figure.
In front of the pedestal is a low stone platform, meant for flowers,
incense, myrrh and other ingredients of worship.

When the play begins, the stage is dark.
We see two indistinct figures inside the sanctum: the Mahout and
the Queen. They are sitting apart from each other.
Pause.
The King enters the courtyard of the outer temple. He has a torch
in his hand.
He enters and sits on the outer steps of the temple. The two in
the inner sanctum are unaware of his presence.
Long pause.

KING: So we begin our tale—
               and in any tale
               the King and the Queen
               sitting on the throne
               should merge into one
               —she on his lap
               become half his royal frame
               or entwined in bed, tangled together
               they must turn
               into a four-armed deity
               thrashing and moaning
               for the good of the land.
               But
               woe betide the times
               where the King sits alone
               outside on the steps
               racked by sighs
               while the Queen is trapped
               in her lover's thighs.

MAHOUT: Who are you?
(*No reply.*)
     Tell me.

QUEEN: Let me go.

(*Pause.*)

Please—

MAHOUT: Go.

(*She moves.*)

But before you go, tell me your name.

(*Pause.*)

Come on. What are you being so cussed about?

QUEEN: Why do you want my name?

MAHOUT: Ts! I told you—

(*Pause.*)

QUEEN: Please, it's getting late. I'm getting worried. Let me go.

MAHOUT: A name. Any name would have done. In fact, most women would have had a name coined and ready before stepping in here like this. But you!

(*Pause.*)

I'll tell you something, you haven't seen me properly yet. I am ugly. Ugly as a bandicoot. I know. But I've had women. Plenty. When I've wanted a woman—needed a woman—my voice has never failed me. Can't remember any names though.

QUEEN: Then why do you want mine?

MAHOUT: After all, it's a matter of courtesy, isn't it? A mere formality. You can't just sleep with a woman and let her go—just like that. So you say 'What's your name?' She gives some name and that's the end of that. But you—the way you reacted to the question—recoil as though I had slapped you. Even in the dark I could feel that. After everything we'd done? God! I'm suffocating in here. I am going to open the window—

QUEEN: Look, I could also do with some fresh air. And it is getting late. I can't stay here any longer. Please let me go. We'll go our separate ways and not see each other again.

MAHOUT: That's why I want your name.

QUEEN: And I won't tell you.

(*Pause.*)

I hope you realize we are both repeating ourselves.

(*He goes and opens the window. She sinks into the darkest corner of the room. The moonlight streams into the sanctum and lights it up.*)

MAHOUT: Nice. The mist's cleared. Nice breeze. It's a beautiful night. Full moon. You can see every leaf in the tree. It's such a bright night, you won't know when it dawns. It'll flow from one into the other, seamlessly.

(*The Queen makes a sudden move to the door and tries to open it, but he is faster than her and grabs her. There is a scuffle. He drags her back and literally throws her into a corner. She moans in pain.*)

Don't. Don't make me angry. You don't know my temper. I have beaten women black and blue. You won't like it. Don't try any tricks. I don't like it.

(*She sits up, rubbing her wrists.*)

QUEEN: It's been lovely meeting you. Every minute of it. And you're ruining it.

MAHOUT: Listen, I could easily drag you to the window and see your face. You know that.

(*Pause.*)

But that won't be nice. Not after the time we've had together. So I say: you want to keep your face hidden? Fine! But tell me your name. I'm letting you off easy.

QUEEN: Let's say, my name is ... Kāmalatāsurasundari.

(*Pause.*)

MAHOUT: Trying to be funny, aren't you? I would have accepted any name earlier. But not now. Now I am curious. Now I want to know. Not be lied to. That's another thing I hate. Being taken for a moron.

QUEEN: I am not taking you for a moron.

MAHOUT: I don't like being taken for a moron just because I am ugly.

QUEEN: Why do you keep saying that?

MAHOUT: Because I am ugly. I know that. And I say it before others do.

QUEEN: I won't say it.

MAHOUT: Surely you have said it to yourself? When you came in here, the lamp was burning, you saw my face.

QUEEN: Yes.

MAHOUT: And what did you think?

QUEEN: I wasn't thinking. I was … just …
(*He waits. She doesn't complete the sentence.*)

MAHOUT: But you saw my face.

QUEEN: I suppose so.

MAHOUT: How did it strike you?

QUEEN: I don't know.
(*Pause.*)

MAHOUT: That's not nice.

QUEEN: But it's true.

MAHOUT: You came in here barely two hours ago. And you don't know what you thought of my face? That's not nice. Not nice at all.
(*He moves so that the moonlight falls directly on his face.*)
Well, you can see me now. What do you say?

QUEEN: If you mean you are not tall and fair with an aquiline nose and ruby lips—I live surrounded by such men and I am sick and tired of them.

MAHOUT: You are avoiding my question.

QUEEN: No, I'm not. Your looks don't matter to me. I came here because I heard you sing. You have a heavenly voice.
(*Pause.*)
I wanted the company of your voice.

MAHOUT: Then why did you put the light out as soon as you came in? You couldn't bear to see my mug while making love to me?

QUEEN: I didn't want you to see my face.

MAHOUT (*laughs*): Why? Are you ugly?

QUEEN: No, I don't think so. People usually describe me in flattering terms. Of course, they don't always mean what they say.

MAHOUT: I wish you would let me see your face. Just a glimpse.

QUEEN: No.

MAHOUT: Look, I am a low-caste mahout, the King's elephant keeper.
(*Looks at his arms.*)
And you? I am probably bleeding all over. There. You've almost scratched my skin off. Such long nails. You are no bazaar woman, I can see that. You are from the upper floors. And you haven't done a day's work. That's for sure. Those nails are for a dainty life.

QUEEN (*laughs*): You're right. They're not used to scrubbing the floor.

MAHOUT: I don't see many rich women. I'm not allowed near them. So it's not likely that I would have seen you. Or recognize you. So why are you hiding your face?
(*She changes the subject.*)

QUEEN: I'm sorry I hurt you.

MAHOUT: That's all right. I liked it. I like everything about bed. Everything. That's why I am good. I am good. Aren't I?
(*No reply.*)
Better than your husband?

QUEEN (*reacts*): How dare you!
(*The authority in her voice surprises him.*)
     He is the best of men.

MAHOUT: Maybe. But what about in bed?

QUEEN: There too.

MAHOUT: Then why are you here?

QUEEN: You won't understand that.

MAHOUT (*aggressive*): Are you saying I am stupid?

QUEEN: No, I'm not. So please don't keep saying that. My coming
     here has nothing to do with my husband. He is a marvellous
     person—affectionate, gentle, trusting.

MAHOUT: And if he's awake when you reach home now, what'll
     you tell him?

QUEEN: I'll say I'd gone out for a walk.

MAHOUT: In the streets? At midnight? And he'll accept that?

QUEEN: Will you please let me go? Please. I'm really getting scared.

MAHOUT: Any children?

QUEEN: Don't.

MAHOUT: Any children?

QUEEN: Don't let's talk about it.

MAHOUT: Why not?

QUEEN (*sharply*): I don't want to talk about it.

MAHOUT (*retreating*): All right. All right.

QUEEN: I want to go home.
(*The Mahout ignores her remark.*)

MAHOUT: I'll accept I am not very good at certain things. Like
     counting. I was lucky I was born in my caste. We only have
     to deal with elephants—and the elephants don't mind an
     ugly, misshapen man who can't count.
(*The Queen hums a tune to herself. It is not 'real' humming as much*

as an expression of her mood. It's evident that the Mahout does not hear her sing. He goes on talking.)

You know why I am so ugly? I was born on a full moon. There was an eclipse. As you know, the worst thing you can do to yourself is to be born during an eclipse. The sun or the moon—the god whose eclipse it is—is already in the grips of the demons. The beneficial powers of that god are weak at that moment, often ineffective. So it's free for all as far as the forces of evil are concerned. A baby about to be born is fair game. It'll be maimed. Or blind. Or even if it looks normal, something will be wrong inside. The brain may be damaged. You won't know till the baby grows up. My mother knew all this and was scared. She was lying there on a torn piece of mat and she heard sparrows chirping. In the middle of the night? She looks up and what does she see? Up in the eaves, a snake had crept into a sparrow's nest and was gobbling up the eggs. She screamed in terror. And I was born. Like this.

(*The Queen Mother enters the courtyard. She has a large silver tray in her hands and on it an object, about two foot high, covered by a saffron cloth. There are flowers, incense sticks etc. in the tray, and a sword.*)

People mock at mahouts. Call us 'low-born'. But where would all your princes and kings be without us, I want to know. What would happen to their elephants? No elephants. No army. No pomp and splendour. No processions. No kings! Ha!

QUEEN: Let me warn you—if we get caught together here, it won't be pleasant for either of us.

MAHOUT: Several times I have asked God—Oh! Do you ever talk to God?

QUEEN: No.

MAHOUT: Believe in one?

QUEEN: No. Though I have often wished He was there.

MAHOUT: But He is there. If you don't believe in Him, who do you believe in?

QUEEN: The Saviour.

MAHOUT: Ah! you are a Jain, then. No God, but twenty-four Saviours! Never could understand that. Who do you talk to when you are lonely—when you are in trouble?

QUEEN: They're all there.

MAHOUT: But no God, eh? Funny what people will come up with. But believe me, there is God. I talk to him. In my village, outside the village limits, there's this banyan tree—enormous—hundreds of years old. And there's our God. A stone. But not on the ground. The hanging roots of the banyan have taken hold of Him and actually lifted Him up. The roots look like trunks of elephants cradling our God. The God of the Mahouts. Sometimes when I am sad, I am lost, I am upset, I ask God. Of course, you can't demand anything of Him. He meant everything to be as it is, you see. But I'm human, so I ask, 'Why have you made me so ugly? Why not handsome, like the Commander-in-Chief? Or the King? Why so ugly?' So God says: 'Are the people laughing at you?' I say: 'No, not any more. Not after I knocked the teeth of a couple of fellows out!' God says: 'Well, I gave you the strength to do it. Didn't I?' So I argue: 'But a handsome face! If I had one, then I wouldn't need these muscles to shut them up!' So God says: 'Would you exchange your voice for good looks?' That puts me in a proper spot. But God knows my answer in advance. 'No, I wouldn't,' I reply, so God says, 'Why not leave it at that?'

QUEEN: You're not ugly, you know. You are lonely.

MAHOUT (*defensive*): I live alone, if that's what you mean. That's all right by me.

QUEEN: That's why you are holding me prisoner. You don't want to know my name. You want someone to talk to.

MAHOUT: I have my God.

QUEEN: God is no substitute—for anything!

MAHOUT (*angry*): All right, people avoid me. So what? They gather to hear me sing. Then they run away. So what are you saying?

QUEEN: That *that* may be a blessing. You can be surrounded by people who are talking—fawning on you—and you can be lonely. So lonely you are terrified. I should know.

MAHOUT: Is that why you came here?

QUEEN: No. I came here because I heard you sing. I had to come. But let me tell you something. Nobody has ever talked to me like you have. Nobody.
(*Pause.*)
I have to go back, but I like you.
(*Long pause.*)

MAHOUT: I think I'll let you go.
(*Pause.*)
Go.
(*She stands up with alacrity.*)

QUEEN: Thank you. I'll never forget you.
(*He strides to the window, almost angry at himself for letting her go. She covers her face with her sari and prepares to leave. He sees the Queen Mother outside. He can't see her full figure, so twists to get a better glimpse of her*).
There's someone there … in the courtyard.
(*The Queen freezes.*)
There's someone … there … outside the main door.

QUEEN: Who's there?

MAHOUT: A woman, I think.

QUEEN: Are you lying?

MAHOUT: If you think I'm lying, go out. See for yourself.

QUEEN: What's she doing?

MAHOUT: Must have just come in. Didn't see her earlier.

QUEEN: What's she doing?

MAHOUT: Just standing there. Still. Like a statue.
(*Pause.*)
She is holding something in her hands, a bundle of some sort.

QUEEN: Is she alone?

MAHOUT: Yes. That's odd. Very odd. I mean—a woman, alone? At this time of the night?

QUEEN: What's she doing?

MAHOUT: That's what I want to know. I mean why here? A ruined temple. Most people would think it's haunted, evil. A wayfarer? At night? And then the traveller's shelter is just round the corner. Anyone would go there!

QUEEN: Anyone else with her?

MAHOUT: I don't know, I can't see.

QUEEN (*scared*): Are you trying to be funny?

MAHOUT: Stop repeating yourself like a parrot. Come and see. Quick. She is about to move...
(*The Queen moves to the window and looks out. Just at that moment, the Queen Mother outside moves out of sight.*)

QUEEN: Where?

MAHOUT: She's come in. Inside the temple.
(*He sees the Queen's face.*)
I have seen your face somewhere before.
(*The Queen turns her face away.*)

MAHOUT: Don't be absurd. After all that we've done together... I mean, this coyness, this fuss...

QUEEN: Look, no one must know I'm here. Please. I must go home. Immediately. Oh God! Is there any other way out of here?

MAHOUT (*laughs*): There's that hole there. If you could fly out, try. Listen, numbskull. This is the inner sanctum. It has a single door.

QUEEN: Please, please, help me. Here—

(*Reaches for her necklace, an almost automatic gesture.*)

MAHOUT (*irritated*): Keep it. If I'd wanted that bauble, I wouldn't have waited so long. That's your estimate of every lower-caste man, isn't it? He's a good lay and all he wants is a piece of gold. I am an elephant keeper, madam, not a fence, selling stolen jewellery. And if someone decides to investigate, I'll get my hands chopped off.

QUEEN: Please, please, keep your voice down. They mustn't know we're here—

MAHOUT: You aren't very bright, are you? I'm sure she is not alone. There must be others. We know there's no God's image here. But they may not. If they are travellers, before leaving in the morning, they may decide to bow down to the deity in here—

QUEEN: I can't stay here till the morning—

MAHOUT: And I don't want to get caught with you, whoever you are. God alone knows whose wife you are. I don't want to—Now listen. Listen! Let's see what they do. Let's see! If they try to come in, there's only one way to stop them. Let them know there's a couple in here... a man and a woman. So if anything like that happens, we have to raise our voices... make noise...

QUEEN: Oh God!... I must get away. Please, please help me!

MAHOUT: For goodness sake, don't start crying now. If they hear you, they'll decide you're in trouble and come to the rescue. People are so bloody nosey these days. Be quiet now and listen!

(*They listen, crouching next to the door, tense with fear.*
Outside, the Queen Mother, carrying the silver tray, comes to where the King is sitting. He gets up and, as though in a trance, removes the saffron cloth to see the object it is covering. He holds out the cloth in such a way that the audience cannot see the object.
He stares at the object and his stance changes as though the object

*has communicated some message to him. He covers it again. Does
namaskara to it.
The Queen Mother, with a nod of her head, signals to him to go
ahead.
He takes the sword from the tray, ties it round his belt, picks up
the torch and walks up the steps.
He knocks on the door. The knock startles the two inside. The
Queen jumps to her feet and tries to run behind the pedestal. The
Mahout grabs her.)*

MAHOUT (*in a whisper*): Don't panic. Do as I say. Do as I tell
    you... Just laugh. Be merry. Come on.

*(The Queen tries to laugh but the attempt ends in a moan. The
Mahout laughs loudly, theatrically. But he is scared. It's not easy.
Knock.)*

MAHOUT: We must pant.

QUEEN: Pant?

MAHOUT: Yes, yes, pant. Heavy breathing. You and me—
(He pants heavily.)
    Let them think something's going on... that we're making
    love here. You see what I mean? Sin in the inner sanctum.
    They'll slap themselves on their cheeks, say what's the
    world coming to, curse us and go away. Come on... Pant...
    heavy...
(He demonstrates panting.)
    Hunnh... Hunnh... Yes. Like that. Come on.
(The Queen moans in anguish.)
    That's it. Oh God! You're good, good, this is heaven. Yes.
    This is... aaaah... Come on. Come. Come. Aah.
*(The King knocks again. The Queen curls up in fear. The Mahout
increases his labours.)*
    Good. Oh God, you are good! uh... uh... uh... You're like
    no one I know... Oh! you are good—good...
(Knocking again. The Mahout yells.)

Hey, who's that? Are you deaf? Can't you hear I am with my woman? Go away. (*To the Queen.*) Come now...yes... Turn this way. That's it... Oh you're divine...

(*Urging her*)

Come on. Moan. Groan. Laugh.

(*The King knocks.*)

You bastard, get the hell out of here. Or else...I'll bash your brains out... Stamp you into mud...

QUEEN: Oh God!

MAHOUT (*to her*): Yes, that's right...

(*Knock again.*)

Bloody hell! Are you deaf? Or are you deliberately asking for trouble? I'll...I'll...

(*Knock again.*)

I said I'll kill you.

(*Knock again.*)

All right.

(*Jumps up. Picks up his stick.*)

QUEEN: No!

MAHOUT: So what do you want to do? Sit here all night while they knock? I'll give the rascals a taste of my stick...

(*Rushes to the door. The Queen, frightened, goes and crouches in a corner. The Mahout opens the door and raises the stick to hit out. He sees the King and freezes.*)

Oh my God! The King!

(*Reels back.*)

Your ... Majesty...

(*The King steps in with the torch in his hand. The torch further lights up the interior. The King looks around for the Queen, while the Mahout quickly ties his dhoti in a knot.*)

I touch your feet, Your Majesty, there's no one here. It's just me! I fall to your feet, sir. Last night a bat entered the elephant stables, so we had to clear up the place. So I came here to sleep. But I am alone, sir, there's no one here. Only me...

KING (*calls*): Amritamati...
(*The Mahout recoils in horror. The King calls again.*)
    Amritamati...
(*The Queen gets up from behind the pedestal and comes out.*)
MAHOUT: Oh...God...the Queen! Forgive me, sir. I...didn't
    know. We didn't do anything, sir. I swear to you. I sang...she
    listened... Her Majesty was about to go back soon...
(*The King goes to her. Pushes back the veil covering her face. Takes
the torch to her face. She recoils. He stares at her. Silence. Dazed,
he looks at her as though he can't recognize her. Pinches her cheek
as though to make sure she is there.*)
QUEEN (*gently*): Please...don't...
(*The King wakes up with a start. He is obviously embarrassed by
what he's been doing.*)
KING (*dazed and without malice*): Is it you? I don't want to
    hurt you.
(*He turns, goes to a ring in the wall and sticks the torch into it.
Then, in sheer exhaustion, leans his head against the wall.*
A long pause.
The Queen moves up to him. Almost in a whisper)
QUEEN: Let's go.
KING: Go?
(*She takes him by his hand and tries to lead him away. He does
not move. They look at each other.*)
QUEEN (*gently*): Why did you come here?
(*Pause.*)
    Why did you? Until he saw you—
KING: I'm concerned about you. You about him.
QUEEN: I am talking about us both.
(*Pause.*)
    Until he saw you, he didn't know who I was. I was just a
    woman, any woman. Now he can gloat.
KING (*spits out contemptuously*): Him!

QUEEN: No, me. For one night, I was nameless.

MAHOUT (*scared*): Madam... Your Majesty ... I swear to you I won't breathe a word of this to anyone. Who'll believe me anyway? They'll laugh at me ... If I speak to any soul, may my tongue get worms in it. Rot and fall away. Please, madam. Please, sir—

KING: Shut up!

MAHOUT: If I shut up, Your Majesty, how will you know? I mean... you must hear me out. You could have me beheaded. Cut to pieces. Trampled under an elephant's foot. But that would be wrong, sir. Very wrong. I didn't do anything. A bat flew into the elephant stables last night, so I came here to sleep for a night. And I was singing by myself. Alone. I do that often. And she came. I didn't know who she was. It was dark. I was sitting here, singing, and she came in and she came to me and—

KING: I said shut up!

(*The King draws his sword and is about to slash at the Mahout when—*)

QUEEN: Your Majesty—

(*The Queen Mother on the steps too suddenly stands up as though she has sensed something. The King freezes, stares, uncomprehending, at the sword. Then almost with a sense of hopelessness, lets it slide back into the scabbard. The Mahout heaves a sigh of relief.*)

MAHOUT: Of course, how could I forget? You are a Jain. You can't indulge in violence. You aren't permitted to shed blood. Ooh! I forgot that—

(*He giggles in sheer relief. Giggling and talking to himself he retires to his corner.*)

Whew! That was close! ... I mean ... how could you draw the sword? You aren't allowed to kill. Huh!

(*The Mahout sits on his mattress. The King and the Queen stand, looking at each other, not knowing what move to make next. Lights slowly dim, plunging the pair into darkness. But we continue to see the Mahout as he begins to drink. Total darkness.*)

SINGER: Memories slide
                 meld and fuse.
                 Discrete moments
                 get flung together
                 strung in a single moment.

(*Lights come on the Queen and the King, acting young.*)

QUEEN: You there! What are you doing?

KING: Don't look. Look away—Don't come near—

QUEEN: You are peeing on our tree!

KING: I say…look away. Wait till I finish.

QUEEN: You are taking too long. You've got your leg wet.

KING: You startled me. I didn't know anyone was around.

QUEEN: I saw you. This garden is only for girls. Who are you?

KING: I am a prince.

QUEEN: Ohho! So you're the prince who's come to be my husband.
    But you are so—small. Don't husbands have moustaches?

KING: I'll grow my moustaches in good time, don't let that
    worry you. You aren't all that big yourself. You are like a
    doll—a rag doll.

QUEEN: If you tease me, I'll go and tell Father.

KING: Then you talk to me with respect. Is that how one talks
    to one's husband? 'You there!' 'You here!'

QUEEN: My maid does.

KING: I'm not going to marry a house-maid. I am a prince.

QUEEN: Good. Then I'll ask you a riddle. See if you can solve it.

KING: Tcha! I have no time for riddles. Solve them yourself.

QUEEN: You don't like riddles? What kind of a prince are you?
    In my house, everybody loves riddles.

KING: Even your father?

QUEEN: Him too. He knows millions of them. Millions of billions.

KING: Why should a king solve riddles? He must rule. He must fight wars. He must make proclamations. He has other things to do.

QUEEN: He does that too. And he knows proverbs.

KING: Can he throw a stone? Can he hunt lions?

QUEEN (*impressed*): You can hunt lions?

KING: Aw! Easy.

QUEEN: Will you show me? I have never seen a hunt. Never!

KING: I know. You are Jains, aren't you? Your kings can't hunt. Your Saviours are all stark naked.

QUEEN (*miffed*): And...and...and my maid says your goddess eats meat.

KING: She does too. But she is dressed in such gorgeous saris. Bright, shiny silk saris. Clothed from neck to toe.

QUEEN (*losing the argument*): Your goddess eats...chicken...and goats...and...and...

KING: But she is decked in gold. What kind of a king is your father? Can't he even afford a jockstrap for your Saviour? Not even a piece of rag to cover his shame?

(*The Queen's eyes fill up.*)

QUEEN: You're making fun of me. You are making me cry. I don't want to marry you. I'll go and tell Mother.

(*He quickly intercepts her exit.*)

KING: Hey, hey! Listen! I'll show you something, if you promise not to cry.

(*Looks around for something.*)

I could show you how to knock a bird off a branch but I haven't got my catapult with me.

QUEEN: I am going.

KING: Show me a bird and I'll try to get it down with a stone, without a catapult.

(*They look around.*)

QUEEN: I can't see any.

KING: It's midday.

QUEEN: Their babies must be sleeping.

KING: All right then, I'll knock a bird down from the branch in the evening. Just for you. Don't tell anyone. Otherwise your parents will be furious. So will mine.

QUEEN: If you show me, I'll let you pee on my rose bush. We can make babies.

KING: What's that? Revolting!

QUEEN: Why were you peeing here then?

KING: Because I haven't had a pee since morning. The front yard is full of guests. So I came here. It's got nothing to do with making babies.

QUEEN: It does too. That's why no boy is allowed to come in here. How did you get in?

KING: I made a hole in the hedge and crept in.

QUEEN: You should have waited till you became my husband.

KING: Why?

QUEEN: My maid says that if a boy pees on a bush and then if a girl smells the flowers from that bush, that's how babies are made.

KING: Really? I didn't know that.

QUEEN: You don't know a lot of things.
(*Suddenly*)
There!

KING: What?

QUEEN: A bird. There!

KING: Ah, yes. Shush now. Be absolutely quiet.
(*Picks up a stone, tiptoes nearer to the bird, takes aim and flings the stone. He shouts in triumph.*)
Got it!

(*They run to the fallen bird. The Queen recoils in horror at the sight of the bird.*)

QUEEN: Oh God! Blood. Poor birdie! It's bleeding.

(*The Queen kneels down and gently picks up the bird. She keeps caressing the bird and whispering to it. The King watches, almost mesmerized.*)

Poor baby! Poor dear baby!... Oh poor thing. Please, fetch some water. Please.

KING: I'm sorry, but it's no use. It's dead.

QUEEN: Dead? No. No. It can't be. It can't be. Wake up. Wake up, poor birdie.

KING: Here!

(*He gently tries to take the bird from her hand but she doesn't let him.*)

We have to bury it now.

QUEEN (*refusing to relinquish the bird*): But why did you kill it?

KING (*not accusing*): You wanted to see it knocked down.

QUEEN: But I didn't want you to kill it.

KING: I didn't realize—I'm sorry.

QUEEN: I didn't mean you to hurt it.

KING: I know that now. Stupid of me—

QUEEN: Poor birdie!

KING (*trying to take the bird again*): Your hand is covered with blood. Go wash your fingers. I'll bury the bird.

QUEEN (*withdrawing*): That was not nice.

(*He accepts that rebuke in silence.*)

You are cruel. You'll hurt it more. I won't give it to you. Wake up, birdie!

(*Runs off with the bird. He stands staring after her. Long pause. Suddenly he calls out.*)

KING: I am sorry.

SINGER: Memories slide,
meld and fuse.
Discrete moments
get flung together
strung in a single moment.
Then the moment
distends, spreads
into years.

(*The King and the Queen are older.*)

QUEEN: And Your Majesty has been urinating on my rose bush again!

KING (*almost shouting with joy*): Really? You are sure?

(*The Queen nods. Holds up four fingers.*)

Four months? Four! Why didn't you tell me all these days?

QUEEN: You know why. (*Whispers*) I waited till I was sure.

(*He laughs delightedly. Kisses her all over. Then suddenly lifts her up and whirls her around.*)

Please—Please—you'll drop me.

KING (*plonking her down on the pedestal*): Never! I love you. You're pregnant! Pregnant! Oh, you're beautiful. And wonderful and glorious and...

QUEEN (*laughing*): Stop being silly.

KING: I am so happy. The entire kingdom will burst into festivities. But first we must tell Mother. She will be ecstatic. This is what she's been praying for...

QUEEN: Yes, we must. She first of all.

KING: Come. (*Calls out*) Mother! Mother!

(*They rush to the Queen Mother's quarters, she blushing, he laughing. The Queen Mother enters.*)

MOTHER: What's it? Why are you shouting?

KING: Mother! Bless us—

MOTHER: You have my blessings. Always. What's happened now?

KING: Happy news. The happiest possible. We're going to have a baby—
(*The Mother looks at him warily.*)

MOTHER: Are you sure?

KING: Of course we are sure.
(*The Mother shuts her eyes and clutches her hands in a quick prayer. The King and the Queen come forward and touch her feet. The Mother lifts her daughter-in-law by her shoulders and embraces her. Smoothens her hair.*)

MOTHER: God bless you! You have made our family tree bloom. May you beget a son whose glory blinds the eight directions.
(*Gently seats her down.*)
Now, the next couple of months are most precious. You need to take special care.

KING: Yes, Mother. She'll be your obedient daughter-in-law.
(*The Queen blushes, laughs.*)

MOTHER: Good. Now I must go to my shrine and celebrate. We must thank the gods for this most wonderful gift.

KING: Yes, Mother.

MOTHER: I'll send you the offering.
(*Goes away. The King and the Queen return to their original place.*)

QUEEN: Yes! Yes! Now I'll show them. I'll show those swine. All these years I have waited for this moment. Prayed for it. Cringing at their glances—

KING: They meant well. They were only anxious.

QUEEN: They were vicious.

KING: As subjects of this land, they were interested in an heir. Fair enough.

QUEEN: Your subjects. For me, they were my judges, my interrogators, torturers—all clubbed together against me.

KING: 'Against' you?

QUEEN: Can you men even imagine what it feels like? To pretend you are unaware of their gaze as they scrutinize the roundness of your belly, the stain on your thigh! Line after line of carrion crows, watching, waiting, ready to caw at the palmful of blood that spurted. And spurt it did—every month—every bloody month. How I hated myself when that happened.

KING: Surely you can forget all that in your moment of triumph.

QUEEN (*suddenly laughs, tousles his hair*): Yes, I can. For you. You could have taken another wife. You didn't.

KING: Of course I didn't.

QUEEN: Sometimes I wished you had.

KING: You did?

QUEEN: Yes, purely for bearing children. Then I could make love to you—for its own sake—to make love. You don't know how I have pined for that. And now I can look forward to it.

KING: You mean it will get even better?

(*They laugh and embrace.*)

QUEEN: You are sure your mother isn't unhappy?

KING: Unhappy! Are you mad? She's wanted a grandson as badly as we've wanted a son.

QUEEN: All these years, she had some hope of getting you another queen. Now...

KING: She'll have a grandchild instead. Look, we can't change her. I can't bring myself another mother. She can't get herself another son. And (*laughing*) I won't look for another wife. So that seems to be a fairly unalterable situation.

(*Kisses her.*)

I wish you would stop being so full of doubts. About yourself. People don't dislike you—

QUEEN: She does. And I can't blame her. Because of me, you deserted her faith—her Mother Goddess.

(*The Queen moves to the window. Looks out.*)

I'm afraid.

KING: Of what?

QUEEN (*points out*): That bit of the thatched roof there. You have considerately built a wall round it to hide the shed. But the roof shows. As though it refuses to be dismissed.

KING: The earth there couldn't take a higher wall.

QUEEN: It's the shed in which your mother keeps her animals. (*Pause.*)

All these years I've been pretending that it doesn't exist. That I couldn't hear the bleat of sheep being taken out at night. (*Pause.*)

For slaughter. (*Pause.*)

You sleep through it. You've grown up with those sounds. I haven't. They often wake me up—keep me awake. But I've pretended I didn't mind.

KING: I know. I'm sorry.

QUEEN: Because I didn't want to hurt your mother.

KING: Why are you bringing it up now?

QUEEN: When your mother says she'll celebrate, what does she mean?

KING (*gently*): Darling, how does it concern us? She doesn't make any demands on us.

QUEEN: The animals are graded according to the occasion. Poultry is offered at daily rites. Sheep, goats for the more important rituals. Then buffalo.

KING: You know that's been the family tradition.

QUEEN: Weren't human beings also offered in sacrifice to the goddess once?

KING: Yes. But that was generations ago.

QUEEN: So you see, a tradition can be given up. Or at least changed.

KING: Mother will not agree to give up her practices. You know that. She feels she owes it to our ancestors. We've been through all this before.

QUEEN: But now it concerns our child. What offerings will be considered worthy of a royal birth, do you think?

(*No reply.*)

They say when you were born, every inch of the earth for miles around was soaked in blood.

KING: People exaggerate.

QUEEN: Yes, you're right. I shouldn't be complaining about the scale. Just the thought. Of bloodshed. Even a single drop of blood.

(*Pause.*)

I don't want it. Not in the name of our child.

KING (*calmly*): I know how you feel. But look at it this way. She has accepted the fact that we will not be party to her violent rites. And she carries them out in her own separate shrine. In her shell. Let's leave it at that.

QUEEN: I don't want to hurt her. She can live by her beliefs. But we are Jains. Our son will be a Jain. He will have to uphold the principle of compassion for all living beings, of non-violence. Should we allow a blood rite to mark his arrival? It would be wrong. Terribly wrong!

(*Suddenly she is overtaken by nausea. The King supports her. She retches. When she recovers, he takes her back to the pedestal. She sits on it. He moves to the Queen Mother's quarters.*)

KING: Mother—

MOTHER: Yes—

KING (*gently*): Mother, please don't get upset. But—

MOTHER: You don't have to beat around the bush. Come out with it.

KING: I want you to promise me that there will be no blood sacrifices in honour of our child.

(*Pause.*)

MOTHER: I was expecting this.

KING: Please, Mother.

MOTHER: You are denying me the right to my worship!

KING (*firmly*): No, Mother, I'm not.

MOTHER: You're treating my goddess as though she were a cheap, tribal spirit. And you are cutting off my path to her.

KING: Try and be sensible, Mother. No one is stopping you from worshipping your goddess or from your own form of worship. But I am a Jain. My son will be a Jain—a Jain King. I cannot have his birth greeted with the infliction of death.

MOTHER: You were not born a Jain. You were born my son. But you betrayed me and my faith. Instead of choosing the woman and bringing her to your faith, you chose hers.

KING: I accepted the faith because I found truth in it and compassion for the world in pain. I don't want to add to the pain. I will not let anyone do it. Certainly not in the name of my son.

MOTHER: He is my grandson too. I too have prayed for him. For me, he is the gift of my goddess.

KING: A king can follow only one path and I have chosen mine.

MOTHER: My feelings don't matter to you. It's mother, ranting and raving as usual. All right. Let her have her way. I'll move out of the palace.
(*The King tries to remonstrate.*)
I shall live in a separate cottage outside the palace.

KING: Mother, this is your home. This is where you gave birth to me, brought me up. We don't want you to go. Please, don't. I am only talking of this one occasion.

MOTHER: My gods have already been expelled from this house and live, shunned and starved, like outcastes. I should have followed them out. But I was blinded by my love for you.
(*Pause.*)
But I want you to promise me something.

KING: Yes?

MOTHER: I shall live away from the palace, in a corner of my own. And there, I shall live as I please. With my gods. My sacrificial animals. No further interference from you two.

KING: All right, Mother.

MOTHER: Promise.

KING: I promise.

MOTHER: All right. Will you arrange to have a cottage built next to the shrine for me? And a shed for my animals? Or should I look to it myself?

KING: I'll attend to it.
(*He turns to go.*)

MOTHER: Before you go, son—
(*He stops. He's been expecting this too.*)
I don't want to be nasty. But I am your mother and it worries me. Are you sure she's pregnant?

KING: Yes, I am.

MOTHER: Have you checked with the palace nurse?

KING: No, but she has.

MOTHER: I wanted to, but decided against it. If she heard that I was making enquiries, she would immediately decide I was doubting her word.

KING (*laughs*): But you are. However, there's no cause for it.

MOTHER: You should check personally.

KING: I'll accept my wife's word for it.

MOTHER: You know what happened last time.

KING: I do. But—

MOTHER: I hope it's not a repetition.

KING: She was still a child then. She knew very little. She was under such pressure to produce an heir. Her period was delayed by a few weeks and everyone went to town about her being pregnant. She too got carried away.

MOTHER: She claimed to be pregnant.

KING: She wanted to be pregnant. She was desperate.

MOTHER: She showed all the signs. Not just the stopping of periods. Her belly began to show. She had morning sickness—

KING: She couldn't have feigned all that.

MOTHER: Her problem is that she has too much imagination.

KING: She is sensitive.

MOTHER: She lives wrapped up in herself. She should listen to the world around her. Open her eyes to it: ears to it.

KING: She's been a good wife. A good queen.

MOTHER: You became the laughing stock of the world. You had to swallow public humiliation.

KING: Not swallow. Face. A king sometimes has to do that.

MOTHER: Soon after it came to light that it was a false pregnancy, I overheard two palace maids, giggling. 'A hen doesn't need a cock to lay eggs,' one of them was saying. 'She can do it on her own!' I could have died of shame.

KING: I hope you didn't dismiss them from service for saying so.

MOTHER: I did.

KING: Tongues won't wag any less outside the palace.

MOTHER: It was your palace. Yours and hers. That's why I couldn't chop that tongue off!

(*The King shrugs. The Mother walks out. As the lights brighten, we see the Mahout, still drinking. He casts surreptitious glances at the King and the Queen. Long pause. The Queen moves to the King.*)

QUEEN (*softly*): Let's go. Please.

(*The King does not respond.*)

MAHOUT: Why are you hanging on here? Why don't you go back to the palace—

KING (*in agony*): Oh God! God! God!

MAHOUT: I thought I was gone, finished, no more life. Now that I have been granted a few more years, I'd like to be left in peace. Go back to the palace.

QUEEN: I swear to you. It won't happen again. Ever. Please.
(*The King does not respond. Pause.*)
    All right...
(*She moves to the door.*)

KING: No. Please. Stay!
(*She stops.*)
    It won't take long.

QUEEN (*surprised, in a whisper*): What won't take long?

KING: I'll tell you. Let me recover. I'll tell you what's to be done.
(*Pause.*)
    Let me get my breath. After all I've been through. Hours...

QUEEN (*taken aback*): How long have you been here?
(*He shrugs.*)
    Have you been standing out there... all this while? Listening to everything going on inside?
(*Unbelieving*)
    Oh God!

KING: What else could I do?
(*As the King speaks, lights change. The Mahout's song begins in the background, not sung by the Mahout but represented by a melody played on a wind instrument by a musician who appears on stage, while the Mahout mimes singing. A beam lights up the King as he relives his agony, moment by moment.*)
    At midnight, he started singing in the distance. I felt you wake up. I felt you slide out of my bed. You got up. Left. I opened my eyes, saw you press yourself against the window and listen. And then, slip away. I followed. Through the biting chill and

you didn't even have a shawl on... You went out of the royal
garden...into the street. You entered this ruined temple. The
singing stopped. Those noises began. Those horrible, animal
noises of copulation. I couldn't ... breathe.

(*The Queen covers her face in horror.*)

I was numb. Couldn't breathe. I needed fresh air. I ran. I
ran back into the garden.

(*The King runs into the garden. Almost breaks out into a scream
but gags himself with his fists. Sits clutching his head. Controls
himself.*

The Queen Mother enters. Sees him from a distance.)

MOTHER: Son—

(*The Queen takes a sudden intake of breath.*)

Son—

KING: Mother! What are you doing here?

MOTHER: You know my prayers finish only at midnight. Tonight
they went on a little longer. The lights. The songs. It was
beautiful. I was on my way back when I saw you. What are
you doing here at this hour?

KING: I felt suffocated in the palace, hot. Needed a breath of
fresh air. So I came here.

MOTHER: You felt hot? In the depth of winter? I'm freezing. And
you should be wearing something warmer.

KING: Thank you. I'm fine.

MOTHER: Don't be silly. Look, even the swans are frozen in the
lake. (*Laughs.*) They could be images carved in ice. Hot!

(*Pause. She notices something is wrong. She goes nearer. He half
turns away lest she notice his state.*)

But you are sweating. And your eyes are bloodshot. Are you
all right?

(*Long pause.*)

Son—

KING: Yes?

MOTHER: What is it? What's wrong?

KING: Me? Nothing.

MOTHER: Don't try to fool me. I know you. The moment I saw you from there, I knew. Even in the dark. There's something wrong, isn't there? Very wrong.

KING: What do you want me to say? I told you there's nothing wrong. I felt like a walk in the open—

MOTHER: Give me your hand.
(*She takes his hand and places it on her own head.*)
If you don't tell me what's on your mind, let my skull splinter into a thousand shards.
(*The King withdraws his hand, as though stung.*)

KING: Mother, why are you hounding me? Why don't you leave me alone?

MOTHER: You are telling lies. You are trying to hide something from your own mother. Must be something really serious.
(*Pause. Fiercely*)
Tell me. Tell me. I can't help you unless you tell me.

KING: Around midnight, I had a dream. It woke me up.

MOTHER: Yes? What was it?

KING: In the dream... (*Pause.*) I saw that the royal swan in our garden had got caught in mud and was flapping its wings.

MOTHER: It was asking for help.

KING: I don't know. I suppose so...

MOTHER: It was caught in mud. Trapped. And crying out for help?

KING: Yes.

MOTHER: Then?

KING: Nothing. I woke up. Felt wide awake. So I came out for a walk.

MOTHER: And you came to check if the swans were all right?

KING: No. Not really. I don't know. Perhaps yes. It was a vivid dream. It felt real.

(*Laughs.*)

Anyway the swans are there, safe, fast asleep. That's all. Are you happy now?

MOTHER: No, I'm not.

KING: I've told you the truth.

MOTHER: I know. And I'm glad you told me. It's a bad dream.

KING: Now, Mother...

MOTHER: It doesn't augur well.

KING: Don't start on that, Mother.

MOTHER: Dreams speak to us. They come to warn us.

KING: Now you know why I was reluctant to tell you about it.

MOTHER: Dreams have spoken to me. And whenever I ignored them, I suffered. Like when I lost your father. I was warned. You know that. I still blame myself. A dream like this is like an epidemic. The longer you ignore it, the more it spreads. Eats into more of the family and the populace. It's fortunate I came to know right now.

(*He makes a dismissive gesture.*)

You go back to your bed. Or wander around the garden. But then take this shawl. Leave the dream to me.

KING: And where are you going?

MOTHER: I'm going back to my goddess. She'll save us.

I know precisely what needs to be done.

KING: What are you going to do?

MOTHER: Don't ask.

(*Long pause. The King waits.*)

There's going to be a heavy mist soon. And you are dripping wet. Go back and change and go to bed.

KING: Why don't you tell me what you intend to do?

MOTHER: I shall offer the goddess a hundred fowl in sacrifice. (*The King has anticipated something like this but cannot suppress a gasp. The Queen, too, concealed in the darkness, gasps.*)
A hundred fowl. If we slake her parched throat, we may yet avert disaster.
(*Lights change: we see the King, the Queen and the Mahout.*)

MAHOUT: I knew it! I knew it would finally skewer me. No, no, that's not right, Your Majesty. A hundred fowl—I know what that slaughter means. It's witchcraft. Whip me, Sir, brand me. But don't don't take away my voice.

KING: Be quiet!

MAHOUT: What'll happen to me, if I lose my voice? I have nothing else...only my songs. Please, please, don't destroy me by taking them away.

QUEEN: Don't be alarmed. I'll see that nothing happens to you.

MAHOUT: Thank you, madam. You are like a mother to me. I'll never forget your kindness—
(*He literally touches her feet.*)

QUEEN (*no irony*): Trust me. I shall not deprive the world of your voice. I shall not desecrate it.
(*Caresses his hair.*)

KING (*turning his face away in disgust*): Bravo!

QUEEN: Spare me your disgust. You take your blood and gore. I'll choose his voice—

KING: Will you at least let me finish?

QUEEN: Yes?

KING: I refused. There was no question of any bloody rite.
(*The lights change. The King and the Mother.*)
Mother, please. Don't do anything. Let things be. Please.

MOTHER: I am not asking you to join in.

KING: I know. It's just—I don't want you to do anything. No
rites. No sacrifices. (*Pause.*) Please, Mother, this once. No
bloodshed.

QUEEN (*from the dark*): Why didn't you tell her there was no
dream? No swan. That you'd made it up.

KING: Had I? I'm not so sure. I was talking about the swan. But
I was thinking of you.

MOTHER (*baffled*): Are you trying to stop me? When I moved
out, you promised that I would be allowed to live on my
own terms.

KING: Mother, you don't have to do anything, because...there
was no dream. That was a lie. I made it up.

(*The Mother stares at him, not comprehending.*)

MOTHER: No dream?

KING: No. The dream was a piece of fiction. So you don't have
to do anything about it.

(*He puts his palm on her head.*)

Here. I swear I made it up. Are you satisfied?

(*Withdraws his hand. The Mother is still trying to make sense.*)

MOTHER: No dream? Why did you say there was one then?

KING: I had to tell you something.

MOTHER: You're hiding something from me.

KING (*suddenly*): In God's name! Is there no way to escape this
hell?

(*The Queen Mother stares at him.*)

MOTHER (*quietly*): If you are going through hell, why isn't she
here by your side? She figures in it somewhere, doesn't she?
That's why you are tying yourself into such knots. At this
time of the night. Where is she?

(*Pause.*)

You are running away from her, aren't you?

(*Pause.*)

Why?

(*Pause.*)

I'll promise you something. On oath. Take me to her now. And I'll give up my faith and become a Jain.

(*Pause.*)

That's what you've always wanted. She has always wanted.

(*Pause.*)

You won't accept the offer. Why?

(*The truth dawns on her. She steps back in horror.*)

Oh my mother! Don't tell me! I knew it would happen ultimately... But don't tell me she's done it... She is with someone. A lover! Oh my God—

(*The King turns away.*)

When? Tonight?... It has to be. You were happy enough with her last evening... Is she in the palace?

(*No answer.*)

No. You mean she is lying between someone's thighs this moment?

KING: Mother—

MOTHER: Oh horrible! Horrible ! Where? Where is she? Tell me—In some hole? A god-forsaken garret? Where? Where did you see them?

KING: Control yourself—

MOTHER: Has she fallen so low? The whore—And you. How can you stand here like this? I should cut her to pieces... feed her to wolves and vultures. Do it, son, now!

KING: Don't be hysterical, Mother—

MOTHER: Throw her bones to the dogs. She has betrayed you. You are not bound by your vows now. All this nonsense about non-violence. It had to go. Let it go. Kill the harlot and her lover. If you won't do it, I'll do it. Let me fetch my sacrificial knife from the temple. I'll—

(*She turns to go to the temple. He holds her back.*)

KING: Calm down, Mother. Please—

MOTHER: What kind of a man are you? You have lost your manhood. You, you impotent...

(*Spits in his face. He reels back. But that action suddenly calms her. She suddenly realizes what she has done. Quickly moves forward and wipes his face.*)

Forgive me. Forgive me.

(*They look at each other. Their deep fondness for each other is clear in that look.*)

I am becoming decrepit—and still I haven't learnt to control my temper.

(*He smiles.*)

All right. You won't shed blood. Then throw her out. Get yourself another wife.

(*He does not respond. Incredulous*)

Surely you are not going to... forgive her? Continue as though nothing has happened?

KING: I don't know what to do.

MOTHER: You love her. But such love is meant for harlots. She has drowned our family in sin. She has called out to demonic forces.

KING: Mother, please. Please, help me.

MOTHER (*gentle*): Do you think I like tormenting you—my only child, the light of my life?

KING: Help me. Please.

(*Pause.*)

I am lost—

MOTHER: We have to do something.

(*She looks at him, deeply moved. Comes to him.*)

You won't offer a living animal in sacrifice.

KING: I can't.

MOTHER: So what if it isn't living? Will that do?

KING: What do you mean—

MOTHER: No, I don't mean a carcass. Silly ass! What you offer
to the gods, you have to partake of. If it isn't living...
(*Laughs.*)
How dumb can you be! All right. There will be no bloodshed.
We'll compromise.

KING: If anything has to be done, it'll be done by me. Promise.
Not you. Nor anyone else. Mother, whatever's happened,
concerns me, my wife. And I need her. (*Anguished*) I can't
let her go.
(*The Mother stares.*)

MOTHER: All right. Go to her. I'll come there with the offering.
There'll be no bloodshed.

KING: Thank you.

MOTHER: Go there and wait. I'll follow you.
(*As though answering an unasked question*)
I'll smell her out.
(*The Mother goes back to the silver tray on the steps of the temple.
The King moves to the Queen.*)

QUEEN (*tense*): And so?

KING (*calls out*): Mother—Mother—

QUEEN (*aghast*): She's here? You brought her here with you?

KING: No. I didn't. She...smelt us out.

QUEEN: If only I knew you, as she does.

KING (*goes to the door*): Mother—
(*The Mother gets up, picks up the tray, and walks into the
sanctum.*)
There. Put it down.
(*The Mother places the tray on the low platform in front of the
altar.*)
Now, Mother. Leave us. Please.

(*The Mother doesn't move.*)
    I'll attend to everything.
(*The Mother goes out of the temple. The King goes to the tray and is about to take off the saffron cloth when they all freeze.*)

SINGER: The hunter,
                   dagger bright but sheathed,
                   back arching, the axe poised to strike
                   but frozen.
                   The dog
                   lunging behind, unmoving.
                   Patterns dotting welcome
                   on the winter's starry floor.
                   Why then suddenly
                   as the mists roll back
                   does my heart tremble
                   at the hound's burning eye?

(*The King takes off the saffron cloth covering the tray in which the offering is kept. The Mahout cannot resist stepping forward to take a look. Amidst ritual materials like flowers, saffron, myrrh and camphor stands a life-size replica of a cock with its head raised and beak open, as though it was crowing. The Queen gasps.*)

KING: This is the offering. A sacrifice of dough. A substitute
    for a live fowl.
(*The Queen stares at the cock of dough. The King, as though to reassure her*)
    It's dough. Inanimate.
(*The Mahout begins to giggle, more from relief than in derision.*)
    Don't you dare!
(*The Mahout retires to his corner trying to suppress his giggles.*)
    Don't you dare!

(*He turns and looks at the Queen. Trying to make it all sound normal, he holds the sword over the cock.*)

All you have to do is place your right hand on the back of my fist. Like this.

(*Demonstrates by placing his left hand on the back of his right.*)

And I'll push the blade into this lump of dough. We will, together. That's all. That'll be the end of it.

QUEEN: This is a temple! You want to violate it?

KING: But it's only dough. There's no violence in it.

QUEEN: But... but... this sword. This plunging in of the blade. The act... it's violence.

KING: There's no bloodshed.

QUEEN: Then why are you doing it? Why? Blood at least makes sense if you believe in bloodthirsty gods. But this... you can't knowingly fool yourself.

KING: It's a small thing. A symbolic gesture...

(*The Queen looks at the King, almost with compassion. He stares at her numbly.*)

QUEEN: You have taken this on to save me, haven't you? To ensure that your mother doesn't contaminate me with her violence?

(*Pause.*)

You are a good man. I have always known that.

(*Pause.*)

Perhaps, I don't deserve you.

KING (*softly*): I want you back. I can't live without you.

QUEEN: Nor can I.

KING: But we can't go back as though nothing has happened. Something has happened. Something terrible. We can't leave it to Mother to handle. It's my problem. Ours.

QUEEN: We'll face it together. But not here. At home.

KING: And take this cock home with us?

(*A new note has crept into the conversation which chills her.*)

QUEEN: Take it home? Why?

KING: How else do we tackle the problem?

QUEEN: I don't understand…

(*Pause.*)

KING: How do we face the problem…

(*He looks at the cock.*)

   … without this?

QUEEN: How will it help?

KING: I don't know. But I have a feeling it will.

QUEEN: How?

KING: I don't know. But when I was waiting outside, lost, adrift, sunk in misery, Mother brought the offering. I looked at it and I felt better.

(*Pause.*)

   I felt help was on its way.

(*Pause.*)

   It sort of signalled to me.

(*Pause.*)

   I could feel the reassurance. Don't keep questioning, it said, surrender.

(*Pause. The Queen stares.*)

   Look at it. Just look. Please. And perhaps you'll see what I mean. I'm sure you will. It's there to help.

QUEEN: Perhaps. And you want to harm it?

KING: Not harm. Sacrifice. That's the whole point of its being there. That's its whole purpose.

QUEEN: Do you realize that those words would sum up my life as well?

(*Pause.*)

   I won't take part in it.

KING (*desperate*): You don't have to believe! Merely carry out the rite. Along with me. That's enough.

(*She shakes her head firmly.*)

QUEEN: Why are you doing this to yourself? You are like a child. You want to hurt me. But you are hurting only yourself.

KING: But I have to do something. And I don't know what!

QUEEN: All right. Go ahead. Do as you wish. If it makes you feel better. I am going home.

KING: But you can't. I can't let you go.

QUEEN: Can't?

KING: Because we are husband and wife—coupled in the eyes of God, joined together with the sacred fire as the witness. We are bound by our vow—to do everything together.

QUEEN: You want me to play your wife so I can damn myself as an adulteress?

KING: Look, we don't know everything about this world. There may be…powers…forces we know nothing about.

(*Pause.*)

Who knows, if we had listened to Mother we may not have lost our child…

(*She looks at him horrified. Pause.*)

QUEEN: What did you say?

KING: I don't know—I mean—what do I—

QUEEN: So I lost my baby because I didn't follow your mother's orders? Because I didn't kill and maim?

KING: I am not saying that.

QUEEN: Yes, you are. Late in my life, I become pregnant and I have a miscarriage—and you are saying that it was a punishment meted out to me for my defiance.

KING: I didn't say punishment—

QUEEN: I lost my baby! I still haven't got over it. You know that.

I still feel devastated by it. And you are now saying it was chastisement for my wickedness.

KING: Listen to me—

QUEEN: A curse I deserved? And all these years—when you were being loving and understanding, the ideal husband—you were only pretending. That's what you believed?

KING: I am not holding you responsible for your miscarriage. But you can't blame it on me or Mother either.

QUEEN: Sometimes I've felt—I had to abort to prove to you I was pregnant. To show you the proof.

KING: What are you talking about?

QUEEN: And I suppose that's why I haven't become pregnant since then. Your mother's goddess in her wrath has made me sterile! And all those years you have agreed with that—God! How I loathe you and your mother and your whole—

KING: No, I didn't. But can you blame me for believing that now? Now—after this betrayal—this treachery?

QUEEN: All right. Go ahead. Believe what you like. But I'll not agree to the sacrifice. I'll never.

(Sudden laughter is heard from a distance. The Queen looks up surprised. The lights change. The Queen Mother enters from behind the pedestal, laughing. She is energetic, ebullient, a dancing, spectral figure, not the person we have seen earlier.)

MOTHER (laughing): Bravo! Excellent! Excellent! More power to you!

QUEEN: What do you want?

MOTHER: We should strip ourselves bare and stand naked face to face. Let us. There's no one else. No one else can be here.

QUEEN: Why have you come here?

MOTHER: Don't agree to the sacrifice. Refuse. Let him plead. Don't yield. That's what I've come to tell you.

QUEEN: What are you up to now?

MOTHER: Me? Why?

QUEEN: This sudden, new tack? Is it some new game? A new opening?

MOTHER: Don't be so suspicious. I mean it. Don't agree to the sacrifice. Don't yield to his entreaties. The more you refuse, the more will my son suffer. Let him.

QUEEN: You've hated me from the day I stepped into this palace.

MOTHER: The only relationship in the world which does not wither and fade away is that of hate. That'll keep us together—at least so long as my son remains a Jain.

QUEEN: I refuse to discuss my religion with you.

MOTHER: I couldn't care less about your religion. It's my son's that concerns me.

QUEEN: You brought up your son drenched in bloody sacrifices, bile and gore. In violence. He was bound to turn away. He's a good man.

MOTHER: What do you know of violence? Or of pain? You seem so averse to blood that I wonder you didn't prefer to remain a virgin. For many years I was childless. Then—one day—I became pregnant.

(*The Queen turns away.*)

QUEEN: I don't want to know.

MOTHER: Of course you don't. You have a fickle womb. False pregnancy! Miscarriage! Mine is made of steel. We were ecstatic. But labour began and the child refused to come out. They said the foetus was set transverse in the womb. For four days and nights I screamed in pain. I prayed for death so my child could live. Ultimately they pinned me down to the floor, spreadeagled, and the nurse shoved her hand into my uterus, twisted him around and pulled him out. I was screaming through the gag they had thrust into my mouth. You couldn't begin to imagine what I went through then. I knew I was going to die. I cast one last glance at my darling son—a farewell look, I thought—and saw him drenched in blood, half-wrapped in my placenta, and I began to laugh. I lived. I drowned him in blood. You, however, are drowning him in guilt.

QUEEN: I'll never agree to the offering.

KING (*in the dark*): Please don't say that. Please.

MOTHER: Twist the knife in his wound. Let him flagellate himself, revel in self-hatred. He is the offering, don't you see? Make him bleed. It'll please the gods.

QUEEN: You disgust me.

(*The Queen Mother laughs. Disappears laughing. The lights change.*)

MAHOUT (*inebriated*): I may be speaking out of turn, sir, but I think you are being hard on yourself. And there's no need for it. I mean, a woman slips but it doesn't have to be for the worse. I mean, take me. I am ugly, I know. People have called me all sorts of names. But I tell you. I have known a few women. They say there are six types of women...

KING (*gravely*): And what about the seventh?

MAHOUT (*stumped*): I only thought there were six.

KING: No one's written about her. While she sinks her teeth into the man and drinks blood, plucks his entrails like strings, the man's head only laughs and sings.

MAHOUT (*laughs*): You're joking, aren't you? You took me in there for a minute, I tell you. I thought you were serious. No, no, no, Your Majesty. You've got to take your life in your stride. That's what I firmly believe. Do you believe in God? Of course not. Stupid of me to ask. But if you did, then you would have had someone to talk to now. To ask for guidance, if you see what I mean. You can't dictate to Him, or demand things of Him. But you can ask. And if I were you, I would ask: 'God, why has this thing happened? What did you intend when you sent a bat into the elephant stables which brought this elephant-keeper into our lives? Surely you had a design?' And God might say to you—'Might', mind you, I am not saying He will—you never can say what God will answer, that's what makes Him what He is, doesn't it? But I reckon God might say: 'Look at the benefits!'

KING: Benefits. Quite right! We never gave any thought to the benefits.

MAHOUT: There! What did I tell you? Talk to God—ask Him—it makes you see things in a new light. The benefits. Now, there's a thing or two I've noticed about your queen.

KING: You have? What kind of thing?

MAHOUT: Touch her here on her shoulder. Rub gently. And you'll see for yourself what happens.

KING: The right shoulder!
(*Goes near the Queen and inspects her shoulders.*)
The right one. Here? I see. I must bear that in mind. I knew that sometimes caressing and pressing her down here—near the hips—that worked like magic. But this right shoulder thing, this is new to me.

QUEEN: Enough, sir. Please, you are making it worse for yourself.

KING (*ignoring her, to the Mahout*): Any other—shall I say, vulnerable—spots, would you say? Erogenous?

QUEEN: Don't you dare. I am not a piece of meat for you to pick and paw at.

MAHOUT: Sorry, lady. Didn't mean to upset you. I meant it all in good humour. Between the three of us, you know. Didn't mean to hurt.

QUEEN (*to the King*): How could you!

KING: What a pundit. A veritable sage. A guru. A man of divine wisdom ... and beauty.

MAHOUT (*reacting*): Oh, don't worry about her sense of beauty.
    She put out the light as soon as she came in. I told you she
    knows what to do.

KING (*suddenly losing patience*): Enough of you. Go away!

MAHOUT: No. I won't. I am not going anywhere. I am staying. I
    came here first. I came here to have a drink and then sleep
    and that's what I'm going to do. Haven't had a moment to
    oneself and then one has to put up with rudeness. I was
    thinking of going. But now I won't. I'll stay.

(*Sits in his corner. Takes out a bottle and takes a long swig.*)

    Yes, one more thing. Why do you carry that sword around
    if you aren't going to use it? Eh? I mean, it's like fangs in
    a sparrow's beak, isn't it? Pretty useless.

    Oh, don't mind me. Go on. Cluck...clucking...

(*Burps.*)

    I'm leaving in the morning. May have to walk for days before
    I get another job. So have to rest properly. Mind you, there
    is no shortage of kings in this land...nor of queens!

(*Laughs.*)

    I'll tell you what. If you want to hang me by the tallest
    tree—make an example of me, you know—why don't you
    make an image of me with dough—

(*He giggles.*)

    ...with dough and string it up. After all, if you find it fit
    for gods, I don't see why dough shouldn't be good enough
    for you.

(*Pause.*)

    Would a man of dough satisfy her though? Goodnight.

(*He covers himself and goes to sleep and is soon snoring.*)

QUEEN (*calmly*): Before we start again! I didn't say it earlier
    because I didn't want to hurt you. But it's the truth.

(*Pause.*)

    I do not regret anything that has happened. I will not disown
    him or anything he gave me.

KING: How can you be so crass? So brazen? You—

QUEEN: Because it just happened. Without my willing it. It just happened. That's all.

KING: And you didn't pause to ask if I deserved it? I who have loved you all these years—above everything—

(*The Mahout's song, that is the music, begins.*)

QUEEN: I was sleeping by your side. His singing woke me up. The song was so—don't know how to describe it. But suddenly the notes caressed me, enveloped me. They carried me away. For a brief moment, nothing mattered. The palace. Me. You. Only the song. I felt like a flame burning bright. Pure. When I came to my senses, I was here. By his side. That's all there is to it. It just happened.

(*Pause.*)

And what happened was beautiful.

KING: No. I can't believe it's you. This isn't you! Why are you doing this to me? Because I blamed the miscarriage on you?

QUEEN (*gently*): No, of course not.

(*Pause.*)

I want to come back to you. I feel fuller. Richer. Warmer. But not ashamed. Because I didn't plan it. It happened. And it was beautiful.

(*A long pause. He stares at her.*)

I'm sorry. If this rite is going to blot the moment out, that would be the real betrayal. I'll do anything else.

KING: Anything else?

QUEEN: Yes. I promise.

KING: There's only one thing I want.

(*Pause.*)

You. I want you back. All this...this ritual...this...this here...all this is only so I can get you back.

QUEEN: I am yours. I'll never betray you again.

KING: Prove it.

QUEEN (*not quite sure*): I will. Let's go back—

KING: No. Here.

QUEEN: What do you mean?

KING: Prove that you'll be mine. Here. Now. In this place. After all, this is where it all happened. Here in front of this... absent God...

(*Startled, she looks at the Mahout who is fast asleep.*)
You promised. Before it dawns. I won't ask for anything else. Come—

(*He extends his hand. She takes it. He leads her gently to where the Mahout is sleeping. Then he unbuckles his sword and turns to her. She stands petrified as he approaches her.*)

QUEEN (*in horror*): What's happened to you? What are you doing?

KING: You promised.

QUEEN: But...but you can't...not here.

KING: Yes, here.

(*He kneels in front of her and pulls her down, gently, almost pleading, to her knees. Then as she kneels in front of him, he begins to undress her. Takes off her pallu. The Mahout moans in his sleep. Startled, she looks at him. The King, gently*)
Don't be afraid. Let him wake up. Let him see. What does it matter? Let the whole world see. We are coupled in the eyes of God. We need not be ashamed of anything. We must strip ourselves of any sense of shame. Become naked like our Saviours.

(*He loosens her hair. Kisses her shoulder. Caresses her bosom. Kisses her gently in the cleft. She shudders. He tries to untie her blouse. Suddenly the Mahout moans in his sleep and she reacts. Tries to get away. But the King has anticipated that. They struggle. The Mahout sits up with a start.*)

QUEEN (*viciously*): Get away from me...

(*She pushes the King aside and rolls away. He reaches out for her violently and then stops. He laughs.*)

KING: The fowl leave us no choice. Don't you see? There's no alternative!

QUEEN: Get away from me.

(*The Queen is trembling with humiliation, almost on the verge of tears. Suddenly she turns to the Mahout on his mat and then looks back at the King, defiantly.*)

KING: Yes, go back to that savage ape—that ugly beast—

(*The Mahout, has been, until now, sitting and watching in a kind of alcoholic stupor. He can barely understand what's going on. Now he reacts.*)

MAHOUT (*roars*): Enough!

(*Gets up.*)

Enough, I say. I've had enough. I won't put up with any more. The insults. The abuses—no more. I've had enough. Now pick up that toy of yours and get out of here. Out! You may be the royalty. You may cut me to pieces tomorrow. But tomorrow's tomorrow. But now I tell you what to do. Pick that up and get out of here.

(*The King's hand automatically reaches out for his sword. But there's no sword round his waist.*)

Stop reaching out for that sword...as though you are suffering from the itch. Pick that up now. Take it away. Now!

(*Pause.*)

Now, are you going to do as I say or aren't you?

(*They watch each other tensely.*)

You won't? Then I'll do it myself.

(*He reaches out for the cock. Then stops.*)

QUEEN: Go on. Go on. Don't hesitate now. Throw it out.

(*The Mahout looks at her. Then back to the cock.*)

Don't be afraid, Mahout. Go ahead. Nothing'll happen to you. You've my word—

(*Pause.*)

Go on.

(*The Mahout slowly steps back.*)

You coward!

(*The Mahout goes back to his corner and starts rolling his mat, wrapping up his meagre belongings.*)

You coward! Didn't you hear him call you an ape—an ugly beast? I'll stand by you. Fling it out—you—you—

MAHOUT (*quietly*): Madam, if you want to plunge your hand into a snake-pit, go ahead!

QUEEN (*imitating the Mahout*): And so the cock scared even our elephant man. Did it? I suppose now I have only this cock to make love to—

KING: Beware. Don't mock it.

QUEEN: Mock the cock? No, surely not. After all, not even that ape could lift that cock. All right then. I'll throw it out myself.

(*She reaches to the fowl, as though to pick it up.*)

KING: Amritamati, please—

(*In the distance she hears the laughter of the Queen Mother. Stops.*)

MOTHER: Twist the knife in his wound, let him suffer, make him bleed.

KING: Don't. Please, don't—I beg of you—

(*She stares, then looks around as though she is waking up.*)

MAHOUT: Listen, the two of you. Stop playing with these things, these forces. Look at those bats—hanging on the roof. Silent. Still. Watching us. Waiting for some signal. Go now. Fetch a witch-doctor. Let him deal with it. Take my advice. These things can eat into you. Go back to the palace. As for me, I am leaving town.

(*Pause. The Mahout stands looking at the Queen.*)

QUEEN (*gently*): I think I'll let you go.

MAHOUT: Thank you. I'll never forget you.
(*Goes out. Pause. The Queen turns to the King.*)

QUEEN: He's gone. The moment's gone. I am making you suffer. We are here. I love you. I don't want you to suffer. (*Pause.*)

I agree to the sacrifice.

KING: You do?

QUEEN: Yes.

KING: Then come.
(*He raises the sword. The Queen places her hand on the hilt of the sword.*)

SINGER:
Fowl, bird, cock of nine new moons,
bless us. Raise us from our darkness,
cleanse us of our sins.
Your curse covers not as words
but as the dying breath of an infant,
grows as the thorny cactus between bleached
rib-cages.
Remove the poison from the seed.
Remove the rust from the blade.
The worm from the flower.
Only you can save us now.
Only you.
Cock.
Divine Bird, help us—

(*The King tries to plunge the sword into the cock when the cock begins to crow.*)

COCK: Cock...a...doodle...doo—Cock...a...doodle...doo.
(*Total silence. The King drops the sword and stumbles back.*)

KING: What's that? What's that?

QUEEN: It's alive. The cock...is crowing. The cock's crowing!
(*Bursts into laughter.*)

The cock's crowing!
(*Kneels in front of the cock. Picks a palm full of grains from the tray and holds it up for the cock.*)
   Here. Have some. Come on. Eat. Cluck...cluck...

KING: Stop it! Stop it!

QUEEN: Come on, please, eat. Have some.

KING (*screams*): Amritamati!

QUEEN: Cluck...cluck... Have some.

KING: Have you gone mad? It isn't alive! It's dough—

QUEEN (*ignoring him*): Come, Cockoo... Have shum...
(*Lallates as to a child.*)

KING: I said stop it—Look!
(*He picks up the dough and squashes it into a mass.*)
   It's dough. Plain and simple! Dough.
(*The Queen looks up at him in sudden hatred, picks up the sword and lunges at him to stab him. She freezes. She stares at the sword in her hand, horrified.*
A cock crows outside. That takes the King by surprise. He turns to the door.
Suddenly, she presses the point of the blade on her womb and impales herself on the sword. Collapses into his arms.
The King holds her, uncomprehending, listening to the cock's crowing. It's dawn.
The Queen is lit by a beam. She stands up and they both sing.)

BOTH: In the World once divided into two orbs—
                  one lit up by the sun,
                  the other, hid in the shade,

                  the orb in the shade
                  opens itself to the light
                  And warmth of the sun.

Night gives in to day.
Death yields to life.
Like monsoons piled on monsoons
So life follows life.

And through the days,
through endless rainy nights
through life after life
we hear the cock crow.